British
Heraldry

British Heraldry

FROM ITS ORIGINS TO *c.*1800

compiled and edited by
RICHARD MARKS and ANN PAYNE

Published for
The Trustees of the British Museum
and the British Library by
British Museum Publications Limited

© 1978 The Trustees of The British Museum
and The British Library Board
ISBN O 7141 0085 4 *cased*
ISBN O 7141 0086 2 *paper*
Published by British Museum Publications Limited
6 Bedford Square, London WC1B 3RA

British Library Cataloguing in Publication Data
Marks, Richard
British heraldry from its origins to *c.* 1800.
1. Heraldry – Great Britain – Exhibitions
I. Title II. Payne, Ann III. British Museum
IV. British Library
929.6'0941   CR1611

Designed by Patrick Yapp

Set in Monophoto Photina by
Filmtype Services Limited, Scarborough

Printed in Great Britain by
W. S. Cowell Ltd.

Contents

List of Colour Plates

Preface

Heraldry is the most colourful expression of medieval society and, although popularly displayed on the stage and in the cinema, little is generally known of the system on which it is based. The purpose of this exhibition is to set heraldry within its historical context and to explain the principles of this fascinating by-way of the medieval period.

The exhibition shows the historical development of heraldry in Britain from its earliest origins until the end of the eighteenth century in the light of recent research. There has not been a London-based exhibition on this subject since the 1930s and the British Museum and British Library collections have never been used to their full extent in illustrating this story. By showing the collections of these two institutions together with loans from various institutions and individuals, the organisers have produced an exhibition which should be fascinating to everyone. The list of lenders is given overleaf; we wish to express our special gratitude to them.

D. M. WILSON
Director of the British Museum

D. RICHNELL
Director-General, British Library Reference Division

Acknowledgements

We wish to thank the Director of the British Museum and the Director General of the British Library Reference Division for their encouragement, and also the Keepers of the four Museum and two Library Departments which have contributed material to this exhibition. We would also like to express our appreciation for the splendid work of the designer, David Burrows, and of his colleagues in the Design Office, Alan Dingle, Will Richardson and Liz Robertson. For conservation we are indebted to H. Barker (BM) and V. Carter (BL), and to the Museum Assistants and Conservation Officers who were responsible for mounting the exhibition. Photographs, except where otherwise acknowledged, were provided by British Museum and British Library photographers Laurence Pordes (BL), Jane Mullane (BL), and Arthur Sharp (BM). Other loan photographs were supplied by the individuals and institutions concerned, and by Giraudon, Paris (Le Mans plaque), A. F. Kersting, London, (the interior of St George's Chapel, Windsor) and the Maurice Ridgway Collection of F. H. Crossley photographs (the Spencer tomb at Great Brington). The illustrations of the Royal arms of England are reproduced with permission from W. J. Petchey, *Armorial Bearings of the Sovereigns of England* (Standing Conference of Local History, 2nd ed., revised, 1977).

We are indebted to those of our colleagues who contributed specialist catalogue entries: Marion Archibald (coins), John Cherry (medieval tiles and badges, the Sword of State and most of the medieval seal matrices), Mirjam Foot (bookbindings), Mark Jones (medals), Hugh Tait (the Treby dish and seventeenth–nineteenth century European ceramics and glass) and Roderick Whitfield (Oriental ceramics); Miss Santina Levey was responsible for the Victoria and Albert Museum textile entries. We are also grateful for information supplied by R. Williams (Department of Prints and Drawings), W. C. D. Bradford (Courtauld Institute of Art), Niels Jessen (Rosenborg Castle), Michael Archer and Anna Somers-Cocks (Victoria and Albert Museum).

RICHARD MARKS
Department of Medieval and Later Antiquities, British Museum
ANN PAYNE
Department of Manuscripts, British Library

List of Lenders

(and catalogue numbers)

Her Majesty The Queen (238)

The Danish Royal Collections, Rosenborg Castle (247, 249)

His Grace the Duke of Buccleuch and Queensberry (262)

The Earl Compton (250)

Sir William Dugdale Bt. (86, 88–91)

Sir Anthony Wagner, Garter Principal King of Arms (24, 50)

The Trustees of the Winchilsea Settled Estates (87)

The Society of Antiquaries of London (72)

The College of Arms (74, 263, 268)

The Courtauld Institute of Art (92)

The Worshipful Company of Drapers (111)

The Most Noble Order of the Garter (239)

The Worshipful Company of Painter-Stainers (81, 85)

The Worshipful Company of Tallow Chandlers (77)

Musée Tessé, Le Mans (1)

The National Trust (Anglesey Abbey, Cambs.) (246, 264)

The Victoria and Albert Museum (15, 17, 27, 28, 68, 69, 79, 92, 100–103, 135, 216, 235, 257, 266)

I
Early Heraldry

In 1127 Henry I of England knighted Geoffrey Plantagenet, afterwards Count of Anjou, hanging about his neck a shield decorated with small golden lions. The ceremony took place on the occasion of Geoffrey's marriage to King Henry's daughter, the Empress Matilda, and was chronicled about 1170 with a description of the shield in John of Marmoutier's life of the Count. Geoffrey of Anjou died in 1151 and on the funeral plaque from his tomb in Le Mans Cathedral occurs a shield of the same arms – Azure lioncels rampant or (no. 1). There is no evidence that Geoffrey's sons bore his coat of arms (although one son is known to have borne a single lion rampant, and another, Henry II, may have borne two), but his bastard grandson, William Longespée, Earl of Salisbury (d. 1226) did adopt a blue shield charged with six golden lions which then passed to his descendants. This is the earliest known example of a shield with a personal device whose later use by members of the same family can be traced. It may be no more than one of many sources from which later generations sought inspiration for the arms they chose (and sometimes changed), but it does presage the emergence of true heraldry as defined by Sir Anthony Wagner, Garter King of Arms: 'the systematic use of hereditary devices centred on the shield'.

Before the twelfth century personal devices on banners, lance-flags and shields are known both from literary sources and from pictorial evidence like the Bayeux Tapestry. Such early devices already have a heraldic character through their use for purposes of recognition, but no case of inheritance has been traced. From the second quarter of the twelfth century throughout Western Europe, even though armorial practice remains confused and contradictory, this hereditary factor is discernible. In this period apart from the Le Mans plaque there is the evidence of the seals. The seals of Waleran, Count of Meulan (see no. 2) bear witness to the use before the middle of the twelfth century of the checkered coat later borne by the Warennes, Earls of Surrey, the hereditary connection deriving from the second marriage of Waleran's mother. Another famous example, the chevronny coat used on early Clare seals (no. 3), was later to become the three chevrons borne by this ancient house. Shields of arms rapidly began to appear as seal devices, not only as part of the accoutrements of an armed knight on horseback, but in their own right on the reverse of these equestrian seals and alone upon smaller seals. By the beginning of the thirteenth century their use was general among the higher nobility. From seals can be traced the changing shape of the shield, early attempts at differencing and marshalling arms, and the introduction of crests, mantling and supporters, culminating in the full achievement of arms in beautiful seals like that of Warwick the 'King-maker' (no. 35).

As the personal marks of their owners seals have strong claims to be the most accurate evidence of coats of arms, but one deficiency they have is that they give no indication of colour. This is the great strength of the other main source for the medieval period, the Rolls of Arms. Colours are shown in the rolls either in blazon (descriptions of arms in heraldic language), or in painted coats. Later copies are sometimes given in trick, that is, in outline with the colours shown by letters. The term 'Rolls of Arms' covers both the relatively rare cases of collections of arms actually in roll form and others that are really books; indeed, it may even be used more widely for collections of arms found in architecture and stained glass (see below).

The manuscript rolls have been classified into well-defined categories by Sir Anthony Wagner in his *Catalogue of English Mediaeval Rolls of Arms* as: Illustrative, Occasional, General, Local and Ordinaries. While our attention is confined here to originals, or at least medieval copies, it is important to remember that considerably more than half the rolls are known only through transcripts of originals and copies made by heralds and antiquaries at a post-medieval date, particularly in the sixteenth and seventeenth centuries. Many of the rolls derive their names from these later heralds who owned and copied them as part of their working collections.

The coats which may be said to constitute the earliest English roll of arms were painted by Matthew Paris, the monastic historian (d. 1259). Matthew Paris used shields of arms in the margins of his chronicles to illustrate events in the text (no. 7). Earliest of all his shields may be the leaf of painted and unpainted arms with Latin blazons in the 'Liber Additamentorum' (no. 6), possibly compiled as a personal reference list to help in writing the chronicles. Matthew Paris was not a herald, although at St Alban's, a favourite stopping place for the court and nobility, he was in a good position to be well-informed. His marginal shields belong to the group of Illustrative Rolls, in which arms are used in chronicles, cartularies, etc., for illustration or decoration and not as separate rolls. The other classes of rolls were compiled primarily as heraldic collections for their own sake. The language of blazon used in these rolls has been reduced to a system in a way which is not found in the descriptions of arms in early Romance literature. This suggests the work of those with specialist knowledge and it is difficult to escape the conclusion that the majority of the rolls of arms were the work of heralds, whether for a patron or for their own professional use.

Closely associated with the heralds is the important class of Occasional Rolls; that is, records of arms of those present on a particular occasion – a tournament, siege or battle. The oldest example of this group is the Falkirk Roll of 1298 known from a copy made by a later herald. This is closely followed by the roll of those present at the Siege of Caerlaverock in 1300 (no. 13). A later example of this class is the (Third) Calais Roll (no. 25). The largest and most varied group is that of the General Rolls. These usually begin with sovereigns of the world (Prester John, the King of Jerusalem, the Emperor, etc.) and continue with the English nobility depicted in an apparently random order. An early example of this group is the Camden Roll of *c.* 1280 (no. 12). The other two classes are the Local Rolls and the Ordinaries. The earliest of the Local Rolls is the Dering Roll of *c.* 1275 which shows a predominance of Kent and Sussex arms (no. 11). A further example is the so-called 'Military Roll' (no. 70), the arms being painted on the tabards and horse-trappers of pairs of jousting knights apparently grouped, at least partially, by county. These rolls are especially interesting as the forerunners of the Heralds' Visitations of counties which began in 1530 (see Introduction to Section III). The last main type of roll is the Ordinary, in which the arms are grouped according to charges, i.e. all the lions, crosses, chevrons, etc., are collected together. Although known in isolated examples elsewhere in Europe, the Ordinary is particularly characteristic of English heraldry. It is essentially a work of reference and as such presupposes a high degree of heraldic development. The earliest extant ordinary, Cooke's Ordinary of *c.* 1340 (no. 24), appears therefore quite late among the rolls.

To the groups defined by Wagner perhaps should be added another category, that of the Genealogical or Family Rolls. The finest of these is undoubtedly the Rous Roll (no. 39), largely devoted to the holders of the Warwick earldom. The Salisbury Roll of *c.* 1463 is an earlier specimen of this type of roll, where the arms are displayed to celebrate the members of a family and their alliances (no. 34).

The other most important class of document beginning from the medieval period is the grant of arms (nos. 38, 41). The origin of the granting of arms is obscure. The earliest extant patent is that granted by Sir William Bruges, the first Garter King of Arms, to the Drapers' Company, dating from 1439 (no. 111), but grants are known to have been made by private individuals to kinsmen and friends, as well as by the Crown, in the fourteenth century. There was too the idea that a man might assume arms at will as long as they had not been adopted by another. This view lost ground to the theory of arms as 'ensigns of the nobility' and from 1417 the Crown sought to forbid the bearing of arms without its authority. The heralds came to be increasingly employed to regulate the use of armorial bearings, their monopoly prevailing over the view expressed by Nicholas Upton and translated in the *Boke of St Albans* (no. 40) that the arms they gave 'be of no more auctorite then thoos armys the wich be take by a mannys awne auctorite'.

From the second half of the thirteenth century heraldry was frequently used to proclaim ownership. Men such as Sir Geoffrey Luttrell wished to put their personal mark on their prized illuminated devotional books by having their arms and 'portraits' painted in them (no. 23). Similarly, domestic plate, liturgical vessels and vestments intended for use in private chapels, parish churches or monastic houses, often bore the arms of the lay owner or founder (nos. 14, 15). Some of the most spectacular manifestations of the late medieval taste for heraldic display are found in monumental art. In view of the practice common from the twelfth century of portraying knightly effigies in armour, it is surprising that heraldic charges do not appear to be usual before the last decade of the thirteenth century. However, chance earlier survivals, such as the Geoffrey of Plantagenet plaque (no. 1), and the armorial shield borne by the effigy of William Longespée (d. 1226) in Salisbury Cathedral suggest that heraldic charges, perhaps in painted form, on funeral monuments may have been more common than can be proved from existing examples. From *c.* 1290 it is rare to find a tomb of a member of the seigneurial classes without heraldic charges. Westminster Abbey has perhaps the single most important collection, particularly of early examples. On the monument of Queen Eleanor (d. 1290), wife of Edward I, the arms are carved in Purbeck marble on the sides of the tomb-chest; on that of William de Valence (d. 1296), Earl of Pembroke, they are of stone and enamel. Soon after the turn of the century, heraldic charges begin to appear on monumental brasses (nos. 19–22), and are found on tombs of stone, alabaster, etc., throughout England in steadily increasing numbers and covering an ever widening social spectrum.

As might be expected, heraldry was at an early stage popular in royal architectural projects. The first instance of a heraldic scheme in an architectural context are the shields of arms carved in the stonework of the nave aisles at Westminster Abbey between 1245 and 1269. Shields also adorn the Eleanor crosses executed some decades later in the early 1290s. St Stephen's Chapel in the Palace of Westminster is another instance of a royal structure lavishly embellished with heraldry.

Architectural heraldry was far from being the monopoly of the English monarchy. One of the most popular fields for displaying shields of arms was the gatehouse. Frequently the arms of the owner, benefactor, or founder, with his family alliances, were represented, e.g. the arms of the Roos family on the gatehouse of Kirkham Priory (Yorks.), constructed between 1289 and 1296. An even more impressive array of shields of arms appears on the early fourteenth century gatehouse of Butley Priory (Suffolk). The thirty-five shields here form a stone version of a combined General and Local roll of arms. Gatehouses continued to be an eminently suitable field for heraldic display in the sixteenth century, as the splendid series of entrances to Cambridge colleges testify. Architectural heraldry was not confined to these, for shields of arms often decorate spandrels of arcades in

Butley Priory gatehouse (Suffolk), early fourteenth century (engraving by S. and N. Buck)

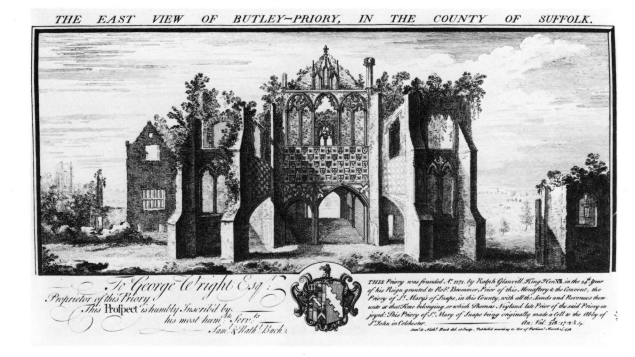

churches (e.g. York Minster), and also occur in the roof-bosses of vaults: a particularly fine series of the early fifteenth century is to be found in the cloisters of Canterbury Cathedral.

Shields of arms also appear in the adjuncts to medieval buildings, in the floor tiles, mural decorations, and stained glass.

With floor tiles we return, as is so often the case, to Westminster Abbey to find the earliest known heraldic examples. The Chapter House, constructed between 1245 and *c.* 1255, contains a splendid set of tiles some of which display the Royal arms of England. During the fourteenth, fifteenth and early sixteenth centuries, the practice of displaying arms on tiles became common (nos. 36, 37). Wall-paintings and stained glass are more perishable than tiles, but there are enough coats of arms portrayed in both media, in addition to the evidence of lost cycles recorded by antiquarians, to show that heraldry was an important element of their design. The high priority the prospective donor of a window could put on the depiction of his arms can be judged from the will of John of Beverley, dated 1380, who left 40 shillings to three churches for glazing on condition that a shield of his arms be placed in each of the new windows. Instances of heraldic glass and wall-paintings are very rare before 1300. Amongst the earliest are the late thirteenth century Royal arms in a chancel window at Chetwode, Bucks., but there are records to show that, in glass at least, shields of arms occurred from the middle of the thirteenth century. Several of Henry III's palaces and castles contained heraldic glass, the earliest being the shields of arms of the King and of the Count of Provence (for his wife Queen Eleanor) ordered in 1247 for Rochester Castle. Only a few years later, at least one of the Virtues depicted in the wall-paintings of the Painted Chamber in Westminster Palace (*c.* 1270, now destroyed), is known to have carried a shield of the Royal arms. From the fourteenth into the sixteenth century there are numerous survivals of heraldic decoration in wall-paintings and stained glass (nos. 27, 28). In churches it often commemorates local benefactors or donors, as is the case with the shields of Thomas Gifford and his wife painted on the north aisle wall of South Newington (Oxon.). In domestic buildings obviously the owner of the house was frequently commemorated, e.g. the fourteenth century wall-paintings with the arms of the Thorpe family in Longthorpe Tower near Peterborough. As was the case with Butley Priory, sometimes the more ambitious heraldic programmes in monumental paintings act as the counterpart of the various categories of the Rolls of Arms. The east window of Gloucester Cathedral can be viewed as an Occasional Roll, for it depicts the arms of noblemen associated with Edward III's French campaigns of 1346–47. There is also evidence of the equivalents of General and Local rolls in glass and wall-painting.

From at least the middle years of the thirteenth century, heraldry played an increasingly important part in all branches of artistic activity. In many ways it can be said to have reached the height of its popularity under the first two Tudor kings. If the Reformation drastically diminished the opportunity for heraldic display within an ecclesiastical context, it did not affect the portrayal of a man's emblems of social status on his tomb, in his house, and on his personal belongings. Indeed, from the mid-sixteenth century onwards new areas for the depiction of heraldic charges were opened up.

1 Funeral Plaque of Geoffrey Plantagenet, Count of Anjou, 1151–60.
Copper-gilt and champlevé enamelled; 630 × 330 mm.

The plaque depicts Count Geoffrey in a mantle and a tunic holding a sword; on his helmet is a lion and his shield bears lioncels rampant or on an azure ground. From the tomb of Count Geoffrey (d. 1151) in Le Mans Cathedral. Probably made in Western France. See Introduction above, p. 11.
Bibliography: Wagner, 1946, p. 6; G.E.C., xi, Appendix G; Gauthier, 1972, pp. 81–83, 327; H. Lardain, 'Contributions à l'étude des origines de l'émaillerie limousaine', *Monuments et Mémoires*, lx (1976), pp. 114–22.
Lent by the Musée Tessé, Le Mans.

2 Equestrian Seal of Waleran, Count of Meulan and Earl of Worcester, 1141–42.
Red wax; D 90 mm.

The checky arms can just be traced on the Count's saddle-cloth (obverse), and on the saddle-cloth, surcoat, and lance-flag (reverse). As the gold and azure checkered shield of the family of Warenne, Earls of Surrey, appears to be derived from this coat, the Waleran seals, which include an impression dated c. 1136–8, have claims to be the earliest known examples of heraldic coats. Familiar to early antiquaries, this seal was drawn by Nicholas Charles (d. 1613), Lancaster Herald (Lansdowne MS. 203, f. 16v), and by John Anstis the Elder (d. 1744), Garter King of Arms (Stowe MS. 666, f. 26v; see no. 99). See Introduction above, p. 11.
Bibliography: Smith Ellis, 1869, p. 179; Birch, ii, no. 5666; G. H. White, 'King Stephen's Earldoms', *Trans. Royal Hist. Soc.*, 4th series, xiii (1930), pp. 62–67; G.E.C., xii, Appendix J; Round, 1894, pp. 47–48; Wagner, 1939, p. 46; Hunter Blair, 1943, p. 2; Wagner, 1956, p. 14. *Aspilogia* II, pp. 26–27.
BL Harley Charter 45 I 30.

3 Seal of Rohese, Countess of Lincoln, after 1156.
Light brown wax; 50 × 75 mm (pointed oval).

The arms on the seal (not on a shield) are chevronny for Clare. The chevronny coat later became the famous three chevrons of Clare, the change apparently introduced by Richard de Clare ('Strongbow'), Earl of Pembroke, c. 1170. Two earlier shields with the chevronny arms are those of Rohese's brother Gilbert de Clare, Earl of Hertford (d. 1152), and uncle, Gilbert de Clare, Earl of Pembroke (d. 1148); both seals (the latter known only from drawings and engravings) date from between 1141 and 1146, making the Clare chevrons one of the earliest known use of arms.
Bibliography: Smith Ellis, 1869, pp. 185–86; Birch, iii, no. 13048; Round, 1894, pp. 44–47; Wagner, 1939, pp. 36–37; Hunter Blair, 1943, pp. 2–3; Wagner, 1956, p. 15.
BL Harley Charter 55 E 13.

4 Armorial Seal of Roger de Lacy, Constable of Chester, c. 1207–12.
Light brown wax; D 70 mm.

The arms are on a pear-shaped shield: Quarterly a bend and in chief overall a label of seven points (obverse); roundel of interlaced ornament (reverse).
The addition of the bend and label by Lacy to the quarterly arms borne by a group of families all connected with one another through Geoffrey de Mandeville provides an early example of differencing.
Bibliography: Birch, iii, no. 11198; Hunter Blair, 1943, pp. 8, 11, Pl. vi b; L. C. Loyd and D. M. Stenton (ed.), *Sir Christopher Hatton's 'Book of Seals'*, Oxford, 1950, no. 71.
BL Harley Charter 52 H 43A.

5 Seal Matrix of Robert Fitzwalter, early thirteenth century.
Silver; D 73·5 mm (ridge and loop handle on reverse).

The matrix shows Robert Fitzwalter with his arms (a fess between two chevrons) on his shield and horse-trapper; in front of his horse appear the arms of Quincy on a shield (seven mascles). Legend (in Lombardic script): +SIGILLUM:ROBERTI: FILII:WALTERI: The presence of the Quincy shield has caused confusion in the interpretation and dating of the matrix. Robert Fitzwalter and Saher de Quincy (d. 1219) were cousins but this seems insufficient to account for the inclusion of the Quincy arms. A more probable explanation is to be sought in their political alliances. Both were joint governors of Vaudreuil castle (Normandy) at its surrender in 1203, and both were associated in the baronial opposition to King John that culminated in Magna Carta (1215). The representation of their shields on each other's seals (a seal of Saher also bears a shield of Fitzwalter, see Birch, ii, no. 6356) most probably represents their comradeship in arms. Found at Stamford (Lincs.) in the reign of Charles II.
Bibliography: Tonnochy, 1952, pp. lvii–lviii, note 4, no. 332; New York, Metropolitan Museum of Art exhib. cat., *The Year 1200*, 1970, no. 333.
BM M&LA 41, 6–24, I.

6 The Matthew Paris Shields, c. 1244.
Vellum; 370 × 223 mm.

A sheet of forty-two painted coats of arms by Matthew Paris (d. 1259), the monastic historian and chronicler, preserved in his 'Liber Additamentorum' (a collection of documents and extracts made, c. 1244–59, firstly as appendices to the 'Chronica Majora' and later as a separate book). Accompanying the coats are the names of owners and blazons of the shields in Matthew Paris's autograph. On the other side of the sheet (f. 171) are thirty-three further shields, twenty-two of them uncoloured. The Matthew Paris shields constitute the earliest known rolls of arms, see p. 12 above.
Bibliography: *Aspilogia* I, pp. 1–2, Pl. I; R. Vaughan, *Matthew Paris*, Cambridge, 1958, pp. 250–53; *Aspilogia* II, pp. 3–10, 36–57.
BL Cotton MS. Nero D.i, f. 171v.

Colour plate

2

5

7 Matthew Paris, 'Historia Anglorum', *c.* 1250–59.
Vellum; 360 × 240 mm.

Ninety-five marginal shields of arms by Matthew Paris appear in his autograph MS. of the *Historia Anglorum*, forming an 'Illustrative' roll of arms. Matthew Paris used shields in several of his historical manuscripts, with other pictorial signs (e.g. mitres and staffs for bishops), to indicate events in the text. The shields or signs are placed upside down when the death of the owner is recorded. In the left-hand margin of the exhibited pages (ff. 130v.–131) shields, reversed, mark the deaths of French nobles ('Dareines', John de Barres, and Henry II, Count of Bar) killed by the Saracens at Gaza in 1240; below, reversed banners commemorate the many Hospitallers and Templars who were captured and slain.
Bibliography: Aspilogia I, pp. xiv, 1; R. Vaughan, *Matthew Paris*, Cambridge, 1958, pp. 211, 250–53; *Aspilogia* II, pp. 11–36; A. Gransden, *Historical Writing in England c. 550–c. 1307*, London, 1974, p. 364, Pl. ix (b).
BL Royal MS. 14 C.vii.

8 Equestrian Seal of Robert Ferrers (d. 1279), 6th Earl of Derby, *c.* 1265.
Green wax; D 64 mm.

The arms of Ferrers appear on the Earl's shield and horse-trappers (obverse), and on a large shield of arms (reverse). The Ferrers arms are Vairy (i.e. Vair pattern but not the usual argent and azure of the heraldic fur), and provide a rare example of a shield of a single tincture.
Bibliography: Birch, ii, no. 5908; Hunter Blair, 1943, p. 7, Pl. vii b.
BL Additional Charter 20459.

9 Equestrian Seal of Henry de Lacy, 3rd Earl of Lincoln, Constable of Chester, 1292.
Brown wax; D 70 mm.

The arms, a lion rampant, appear on the Earl's shield and horse-trapper (obverse), and on a shield suspended by a strap from a tree and supported by two rampant lions (reverse).

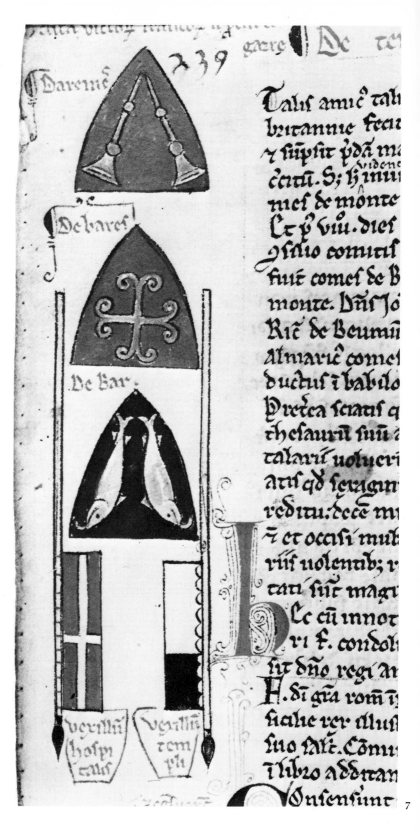

Henry De Lacy adopted the lion rampant in place of the quarterly Lacy coat (no. 4), perhaps in allusion to the arms of his wife Margaret Longespée. In the Siege of Caerlaverock roll (no. 13), he appears leading the van bearing a banner of saffron silk with a lion rampant purpure ('*Baner out de un cendal safrin O un lioun rampant purprin*').
Bibliography: Birch, ii, no. 6156; *Aspilogia* II, p. 116.
BL Additional Charter 15310.

10 Inlaid Tile with the Arms of Clare, thirteenth century.
W 135 mm.

One of a series of armorial tiles laid in the east end of Hailes Abbey church (Glos.), which was rebuilt between 1271 and 1277. The Abbey was founded by Richard Earl of Cornwall, brother of Henry III. His second son, Edmund, married Margaret de Clare in 1272.
Bibliography: Baddeley, 1908, fig. 2.
BM M&LA tile no. 4277.

11 Dering Roll, fifteenth century copy.
Vellum; 3·01 × 0·26 m.

A 'Local' roll of arms compiled as a facsimile copy of an earlier roll of *c.* 1275 (now in the possession of Sir Anthony Wagner, Garter Principal King of Arms). The arms are mostly those of Kentish and Sussex families, and may relate to the rota system for castle-guard at Dover castle.
Both the early roll and the fifteenth-century copy derive their name from a seventeenth-century owner, Sir Edward Dering (d. 1644), the Kentish antiquary and politician, who has inserted the coat of a fictitious ancestor 'Ric. fiz Dering' on both rolls.
Bibliography: *Aspilogia* I, pp. xx, 15, Pl. II; Denholm-Young, 1965, pp 65–89; Wright, 1973, pp. 5, 9, Pl. 4.
BL Additional MS. 38537.

12 The Camden Roll, *c.* 1280.
Vellum; 1·59 × 0·157 m.

One of the earliest surviving General rolls of arms, painted with 270 shields of emperors, kings, and

foreign and English nobility. On the dorse are blazons, in French, of 185 of the coats in a contemporary, or near contemporary hand. Before entering the collection of Sir Robert Cotton the roll belonged to William Camden (d. 1623), antiquary and Clarenceux King of Arms (see no. 81), from whom it derives its name.
Bibliography: Aspilogia I, pp. 16–18; Denholm-Young, 1965, pp. 46, 62–63, 78; Aspilogia II, p. 266; Brault, 1972, p. xx, Pl. 3; Brault, 1973, pp. 8–9, 68–76; Wright, 1973, pp. 8–9, 12.
BL Cotton Roll XV. 8.

13 Caerlaverock Poem (or Roll),
c. 1300.
Vellum; 210 × 150 mm.

This poem, in northern French rhymed couplets, describes the nobles and knights present at Edward I's siege of Caerlaverock castle near Dumfries in July 1300 and the arms they bore. The in-clusion of blazons of 106 coats of arms makes the poem an Occasional roll of arms. A valuable source for the early history of heraldry, the poem includes descriptions of a dispute over the right to bear arms, a change in armorial bearings, and a mention of canting arms.
Bibliography: Aspilogia I, pp. 29–34; Aspilogia II, p. 267; N. Denholm-Young, 'The Song of Caerlaverock and the Parliamentary Roll of Arms as Found in Cott. MS. Calig. A. XVIII in The British Museum', *Proc. Brit. Acad.*, xlvii (1962), pp. 251–62; Denholm-Young, 1965, pp. 16, 55, 59–60; G. J. Brault, 'Heraldic Terminology and Legendary Material in the Siege of Caerlaverock (*c.* 1300), '*Romance Studies in Memory of Edward Billings Ham*, Hayward, California, 1967, pp. 15–20; id., 'The Hatton-Dugdale Facsimile of the Caerlaverock Poem', *Scriptorium*, xxiv (1970), pp. 47–50, Pls. 14, 15; Brault, 1973, pp.

11–12, 101–25; Wright, 1973, pp. 5, 8, Pl. 1.
BL Cotton MS. Caligula A. xviii, ff. 23v–30v.

14 Casket with Arms of England and France, 1299–1307.
Silver-gilt (the gilding and feet not original); 72 × 85 × 42 mm.

The sides and ends are decorated with traceried windows, the crested lid bears the arms of England dimidiating France ancient, differenced on the hinged side by a label of three points overall. Traces of a tripartite division on the inside suggest that the casket may have been a chrismatory.
The arms represent the marriages of Margaret, daughter of King Philip III of France, to Edward I, and of Isabel, daughter of Philip IV of France, to Prince Edward (later Edward II). Probably made in England.

Bibliography: W. S. Walford, 'Some Remarks on a Casket at Goodrich Court', *Arch. J.*, xiii (1856), pp. 134–38; Ottawa, 1972, no. 48. BM M&LA 72, 12–16, 1.

Colour plate

15 Casket of the Valence Family, c. 1300.

Copper-gilt and champlevé enamelled; 95 × 178 × 133 mm.

The casket bears the arms of Valence (see no. 16), England (pre-1340), Brittany (Dreux), Angoulême, Brabant and Lacy. It belonged either to William de Valence, styled but never created Earl of Pembroke (d. 1296), or his son Aymer (d. 1324). On the heraldic evidence the casket can be dated between 1290 and 1320. As is also shown by the tomb of Aymer de Valence in Westminster Abbey, the family were fond of associating with their arms those of the royal and noble houses to which they were related.

The casket is usually considered to have been made at Limoges (France), but recently an English origin has been suggested.

Bibliography: Ottawa, 1972, no. 51; Gauthier, 1972, no. 143.

Lent by the Victoria and Albert Museum (Dept. of Metalwork no. M.4-1865).

16 Heraldic Pendant with the Arms of Valence, before 1324.

H 40 mm.

The shield-shaped pendant bears the enamelled arms of the Valence family, Earls of Pembroke (Barry of twelve argent and azure an orle of six martlets gules). The last Valence Earl of Pembroke was Aymer (d. 1324).

Found near Mitcham Green (Surrey) in 1909.

Bibliography: G. Clinch, 'Armorial Pendant found at Mitcham', *Surrey Arch. Colls.* (1910), p. 212. BM M&LA 1947, 10–7, 1. (Gift of Miss Winifred Rogers)

17 Embroidered 'Opus Anglicanum' Stole, 1290–1340.

Silver-gilt, silver thread and coloured silks in plait stitch and couching on linen; 2·72 × 0·57 m.

Among the numerous shields of arms are those of Percy, Bardolph, Latimer, Roos, Blount, Bassingbourne and Grandisson. The shields are alternately azure and gules suggesting that they were chosen for their decorative effect.

Bibliography: A. G. I. Christie, *English Medieval Embroidery*, Oxford, 1938, no. 76; Victoria and Albert Museum exhib. cat., *Opus Anglicanum*, London, 1963, no. 42.

Lent by the Victoria and Albert Museum (Dept. of Textiles no. T.343-1921).

19

20

22

18 Triptych of John De Grandisson, Bishop of Exeter (1327–69).
Ivory; 239 × 205 mm.

In the centre are the Crucifixion and Coronation of the Virgin; on the wings are (l) SS. Stephen and Peter, (r) SS. Thomas Becket and Paul, with the arms of Bishop Grandisson (Paly, on a bend a mitre between two eagles displayed) repeated twice. One of a small group of ivories made in England by a single workshop for Bishop Grandisson, *c*. 1340–50.
Bibliography: Dalton, 1909, no. 245, Pl. LIV; M. H. Longhurst, *English Ivories*, London, 1926, pp. 44–47, No. LX; J. Evans, *English Art 1307–1461*, Oxford, 1949, pp. 49–51; L. Stone, *Sculpture in Britain the Middle Ages*, Harmondsworth, 1955, pp. 173–74; D. A. Porter, *Ivory Carving in Later Medieval England 1200–1400*, (State University of New York at Binghamton, unpublished Ph.D. thesis, 1974), Chap. IV.
BM M&LA 61, 4–16, 1.

19 Coloured Rubbing of Brass of Sir John d'Aubernoun, *c*. 1320–30.
2·08 × 0·62 m.

The figure is clad in chainmail and surcoat with his feet resting on a lion. On his shield and pennon are his arms (Azure a chevron or). The rubbing was made in the mid-nineteenth century from the original brass in Stoke d'Abernon church (Surrey), by the Revd Henry Addington, vicar of Langford (Beds.). Traditionally considered to be the earliest surviving English brass, recent studies have assigned it to the third decade of the fourteenth century.
Bibliography: Druitt, 1906, pp. 145–48; Macklin, 1913, p. 15; Stephenson, 1926, p. 497; Waller, 1975, p. xi.
BL Additional MS. 32490 B(1).

20 Coloured Rubbing of Brass of a Trumpington Knight.
2·05 × 0·68 m.

The figure is cross-legged, in chain-mail, surcoat and ailettes. His feet rest on a dog, his head on a helmet. Shield and ailettes bear crusilly two trumpets, a punning or canting reference to the Trumpington family. The ailettes also bear a label of five points, added later. Rubbing made by Addington from the original brass in Trumpington church (Cambs.). For long the brass was thought to commemorate Sir Roger de Trumpington (d. 1289). Recently it has been suggested that it was made for his son Giles in the early fourteenth century, but was appropriated for the monument of Giles's son Roger, who predeceased his father in 1326.
Bibliography: Druitt, 1906, pp. 145–48; Macklin, 1913, p. 18; Stephenson, 1926, p. 66; S. D. T. Spittle, 'The Trumpington Brass', *Arch. J.*, cxxvii (1971), pp. 223–27.
BL Additional MS. 32490 B (2).

21 Coloured Rubbing of Brass of Sir William de Setvans (?),
c. 1320–30.
2·05 × 0·68 m.

The figure is cross-legged, in chain-mail, ailettes and surcoat. The shield, ailettes and surcoat bear winnowing fans or vanes, an example of punning or canting arms. Rubbing made by Addington from the original brass in Chartham church (Kent). Formerly considered to commemorate Sir Robert de Setvans (d. 1306), its close stylistic affinity with the de Bures brass (no. 22) suggests it was executed for his son Sir William (d. 1322).
Bibliography: Druitt, 1906, pp. 145–49; Macklin, 1913, pp. 19–21; Stephenson, 1926, pp. 215–16; Waller, 1975, p. xii.
BL Additional MS. 32490 B (4).

22 Coloured Rubbing of Brass of Sir Robert de Bures, *c*. 1330.
2·1 × 0·63 m.

The figure is cross-legged, in chain-mail and surcoat. His shield bears Ermine on a chief indented three (one invisible) lions rampant. Rubbing made by Addington from the original brass in Acton church (Suffolk). For long dated to 1302, it has recently been shown that Robert de Bures only held the manor of Acton Hall from 1310. He died in 1331.

Bibliography: Druitt, 1906, pp.
145–49; Macklin, 1913, pp. 18–
19; Stephenson, 1926, p. 446;
J. C. Ward, 'Sir Robert de Bures',
Trans. Mon. Brass Soc., x (1963–8),
pp. 144–50.
BL Additional MS. 32490 B (3).

23 Luttrell Psalter, *c.* 1320–40.
Vellum; 360 × 245 mm.

The illuminated miniature shown
has Sir Geoffrey Luttrell (d. 1345) of
Irnham (Lincs.) for whom the
Psalter was made, mounted and
displaying the Luttrell arms (Azure
a bend between six martlets argent)
on his surcoat, ailettes and the fan-
crest, trapper and saddle of his
horse. Luttrell arms also appear on
the pennon and the fan-crest of the
helmet handed to him by his wife,
Agnes Sutton (d. 1340), who wears
a heraldic gown of the Luttrell arms
impaling those of Sutton (Or a lion
rampant vert), and on the shield
held by his daughter-in-law dressed
in a gown of Luttrell impaling
Scrope of Masham (Azure a bend or
a label of five points argent, of
which only three are visible). Sir
Geoffrey's son and heir, Sir Andrew
Luttrell, and a younger son,
Geoffrey, married Beatrice and
Constance Scrope, daughters of Sir
Geoffrey le Scrope, in a joint
marriage ceremony (1320); it is
presumably the elder, wife of the
heir, who appears here.
Bibliography: E. G. Millar, *The
Luttrell Psalter*, London, 1932, pp.
2–3, 48, Pl. 157 and col. frontis-
piece; Wagner, 1946, pp. 29–30;
Rickert, 1965, pp. 132–34.
BL Additional MS. 42130.

24 Cooke's Ordinary, *c.* 1340.
Vellum roll; 4·7 × 0·265 m. (im-
perfect).

Painted shields of arms of English
lords and knights arranged as an
Ordinary (i.e. by charges), beginning
with crosses, lions, eagles, etc. The
arms of bannerets are painted on
rectangular banners. This is the
earliest known English Ordinary; its
name derives from a later owner,
Robert Cooke, Clarenceux King of
Arms 1567–93 (see no. 223). See
p. 13 above.

Bibliography: Aspilogia I, pp. xv, 54,
58–59, Pl. V.
Lent by Sir Anthony Wagner, Garter
Principal King of Arms.

25 Third Calais Roll, early fifteenth
century.
Vellum; 2·54 × 0·19 m.

An Occasional roll containing
twenty-four shields of arms of those
who perished at the siege of Calais
(1345–8). The arms appear beneath
a genealogy of English sovereigns
ending with biographical notices of
the children of Henry IV. The Calais
shields begin with the title 'Theys be
the names of the lordes and captens
that weyr sleyn and dront on the
sey at the sege of Callas, wth mony
a man mo of worschip . . .'
Bibliography: Aspilogia I, p. 61.
BL Additional MS. 29502.

**26 Seal of Sir Thomas de Holand,
K.G., 2nd Earl of Kent,** 1353.
Red wax (the shield coated in black
wax); D 40 mm.

The seal displays a plain sable shield
suspended from a tree; on either
side is a mantled helmet surmounted
by a coronet from which rises a
plume of peacock feathers. Sir
Thomas adopted a plain black
shield in place of the Holand family
arms (Azure fleuretty a leopard
rampant argent) which he had used
earlier. Shields of a single tincture,
although very rarely held by
historical personages, were popular
in medieval epics and romances. It
may therefore have been a desire to
imitate the unknown 'Black Knight'
of literature that made Sir Thomas
adopt these arms. The black wax
coating the shield was partly removed in 1825 to confirm that a
plain shield was intended and no
other impression concealed.
Bibliography: Hunter Blair, 1943,
pp. 9–10; Brault, 1972, pp. 32,
36, 54.
BL Seal no. cxcvii. 2.

**27 Shield of Arms of the Percy
Family,** early fourteenth century.
Stained glass; 203 × 172 mm.

The shield is set on a red ground
and bears Or a lion rampant azure.

Since the late fourteenth century
the Percys have been Earls of
Northumberland.
Lent by the Victoria and Albert
Museum (Dept. of Ceramics no.
C.203-1912).

28 Shield of Arms of John of Gaunt,
late fourteenth century.
Stained glass; 293 × 229 mm.

The shield bears Quarterly, 1 and 4,
Gules a castle or, 2 and 3, Argent
a lion rampant sable (Castile and
Leon) impaling Quarterly, France
ancient and England with a label of
three points ermine; above the
shield is blue 'seaweed' pattern
diapering.
John of Gaunt (1340–99), fourth
son of Edward III, assumed the title
of King of Castile and Leon in 1372,
a few years after his marriage with
Constance, daughter and co-heiress
of Peter I, King of Castile and Leon.
Bibliography: Rackham, 1936, pp.
42–43, Pl. 18.
Lent by the Victoria and Albert
Museum (Dept. of Ceramics no.
6911-1860).

29 Willement's Roll, late fifteenth
or early sixteenth century.
Vellum; 9·1 × 0·29 m.

General roll of arms named from its
first editor, Thomas Willement
(d. 1871), the heraldic antiquary
and stained glass artist, containing
painted shields of arms (within
garters) of the Founder-Knights of
the Order of the Garter, and of the
nobility and gentry in the reign of
Richard II (a few *temp.* Edward III).
At the foot of the coats of the
Founder-Knights, the crowned and
gartered shield of Richard II is
placed alone, introducing the 580
shields of the roll proper. Compiled
from an earlier roll made between
1392 and 1397 the manuscript
forms part of the prolific output of
the studio of Sir Thomas
Wriothesley, Garter King of Arms
1505–34, whose index to the
coats of arms in the roll appears in
no. 34.
Bibliography: T. Willement, *A Roll of
Arms of the Reign of Richard II*,
London, 1834; *Aspilogia* I, pp.
71–72; C. E. Wright, 'Willement's

27

30

Roll', *Brit. Mus. Quart.*, xix (1954), p. 49, Pl. 17; H. S. London, 'Willement's Roll', *The Coat of Arms*, iv (1956–57), pp. 153–54; *Aspilogia* II, p. 270; Wright, 1973, pp. 4, 9, 24, Pl. II.
BL Egerton MS. 3713.

30 Thomas Jenyns' Book, *c.* 1440. Paper; 282 × 212 mm.

Painted coats of arms, arranged for the most part as an Ordinary, with bearers' names and blazons of the shields above in French. The arms are mainly those of the English nobility and gentry but include some foreign royal and noble coats. A transcript of the roll was made by Robert Glover, Somerset Herald, in 1578 (Stowe MS. 696) from a copy (possibly the present MS.) given to him by a gentleman of the household of Henry, Earl of Huntingdon, a certain 'Thomas Jenyns', from whom the roll is named. It once belonged to Margaret of Anjou, Queen Consort of Henry VI, 1445–82, whose arms have been added on a large shield at the beginning. Inscriptions and indexes reveal the use and owner-ship of many later heralds.
Bibliography: *Aspilogia* I, pp. 73–75, Pl. VI; *Aspilogia* II, p. 270; Wright, 1973, pp. 5, 9, 17, Pl. 5.
BL Additional MS. 40851.

31 Portcullis' Book, *c.* 1440. Paper; 200 × 140 mm.

Three contemporary, but separate, rolls of arms are contained in this book, which takes its name from the inscription 'Portcullis' (? a reference to a subsequent heraldic owner), written in a later hand at the head of the third roll (f. 56). The general collection of painted shields which comprises the third roll (exhibited here) begins with shields illustrating twenty-eight different crosses and twenty types and postures of lions. Descriptions or names are given in English above the shields.
Bibliography: *Aspilogia* I, p. 90; Wright, 1973, pp. 5, 11, Pl. 6.
BL Harley MS. 521.

32 Miniature showing Sir William Oldhall, mid-fifteenth century.
Vellum; 240 × 160 mm.

Sir William kneels in prayer at a draped lectern before St George, who is rescuing the princess from the dragon. On Sir William's tabard and on the shield filling the capital initial 'G' below are his arms: Gules a lion rampant ermine. Sir William Oldhall (d. 1460) was Speaker in the Parliament of 1450–51. This Book of Hours was executed for him by a French illuminator.
Bibliography: Wright, 1973, pp. 5, 20, Pl. 9.
BL Harley MS. 2900, f. 55.

33 Nicholas Upton (d. 1457), 'De Studio Militari', *c.* 1450.
Vellum; 350 × 220 mm.

A treatise on the rules of war, duties of heralds, etc., compiled *c.* 1446 by Nicholas Upton, Fellow of New College, Oxford, and dedicated by him to Humphrey, Duke of Gloucester (d. 1447). This copy was made for Sir Edmund Rede (d. 1467) of Boarstall (Bucks.), whose arms appear in an illuminated capital at the beginning.
Bibliography: E. Bysshe, *Nicholas Uptoni de Studio Militari Libri Quatuor . . .*, London, 1654; Wright, 1973, pp. 5, 14, Pl. 8; Dennys, 1975, pp. 79–80, 215.
BL Cotton MS. Nero C.iii.

34 Salisbury Roll Copy, *temp.* Richard III.
Paper; 400 × 290 mm.

Leaf from a copy, 1483–85, of the Salisbury Roll of Arms (*c.* 1463), containing painted full-length figures of successive Earls of Salisbury and their kin. The figures shown are Edmund d'Arundel and Sibyl, daughter of William Earl of Salisbury.
The original vellum roll (now cut up and bound into Writhe's Garter Book, no. 262) begins with Richard I and his illegitimate half-brother William Longespée, Earl of Salisbury, and ends with Sir Thomas Neville (d. 1460) and his wife Maud. Most of the figures are in pairs linked by a cord or chain; the men in armour with tabards of their arms and

helms bearing their crests, the women in heraldic mantles displaying either their personal arms or those of both their husband and father. The roll strongly emphasizes the Salisbury connection with Bisham Priory (Berks.) (see no. 46), and may have been made at the time of the elaborate funeral ceremony at Bisham in 1463 when Warwick the 'Kingmaker' (d. 1471) transferred there the remains of his father, Richard, Earl of Salisbury, and brother Sir Thomas Neville (both killed 1460). These three with their wives are the last figures on the roll.
This later fifteenth-century copy forms part of the large manuscript collections of Sir Thomas Wriothesley, Garter King of Arms (1505–34). It is incomplete, but seven leaves are in Writhe's Garter Book (no. 262), and the three leaves in the present volume are now re-united with three further leaves recently acquired by the British Library.
Bibliography: R. Flower, 'The Wriothesley Manuscripts', *Brit. Mus. Quart.*, xii (1937–8), pp. 82–85, Pl. xxxii; *Aspilogia* I, pp. 104, 123; Wright, 1973, pp. 6, 25, Pl. 13.
BL Additional MS. 45133, f. 55.

35 Seal of Richard Neville, Earl of Warwick and Salisbury, 1465.
Red wax; D 80 mm.

Seal on a general quitclaim from Richard Neville (the 'Kingmaker'), Earl of Warwick and Salisbury, to John Ottyr signed 'R. Warrewyk'. The elaborate achievement of arms on the seal shows in the marshalling, supporters and crests, the combination of the Kingmaker's paternal earldom of Salisbury with his wife's earldom of Warwick. On the shield are four grand quarters: (1) Beauchamp quartering Clare, (2) Montagu quartering Monthermer, (3) Neville with a label, (4) Beaumont quartering Despencer. Supporters are the muzzled bear of Warwick (dexter) and the griffin of Salisbury (sinister); the two crests are the swan's head

35

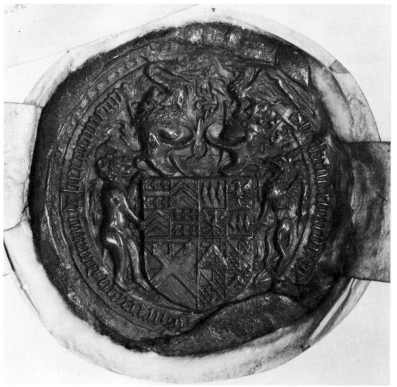

36   37

crest of the Earl of Warwick (dexter) and sitting griffin of the Earl of Salisbury (sinister).
Bibliography: J. H. Round, 'The Arms of the Kingmaker', *The Ancestor,* iv (1903), pp. 143–47; *Hist. MSS. Com.,* 14th Rep. App. ix, p. 270; G.E.C., xii, pt. ii, p. 386.
BL Additional Charter 74449.

36 Inlaid Tile with the Arms of Beauchamp, late fifteenth century.
W 142 mm.

Canynges/Bristol type. This tile from a four-tile pattern has the arms of Beauchamp (a fess between six cross crosslets) set diagonally within a cusped circle. These arms in different designs were popular in the Midlands and the West Country. This design is also known from Great Malvern Priory church and the kiln site at Lenton Priory.
Bibliography: Nichols, 1845, no. 63; Hobson, 1903, no. A 269; H. H. Swinnerton and others, 'The medieval tile works of Lenton Priory', *Thoroton Society Trans.,* lix (1955) pp. 84–97.
BM M&LA tile no. 11,453.

37 Inlaid Tile with Arms of Berkeley, late fifteenth century.
W 120 mm.

Canynges/Bristol type. This tile is said to be from Gloucester Cathedral. The arms of Berkeley (a chevron between ten crosses formy) in different designs were popular in the Severn Valley. Other sites on which they occur are Bristol (White Lion Inn), Tewkesbury, Gloucester and Neath Abbey.
Bibliography: L. A. S. Butler, 'Medieval Floor Tiles at Neath Abbey', *Arch. Cambrensis,* cxxii (1973), pp. 154–58.
BM M&LA tile no. 2139.

38 Edward IV's Grant of Arms to Louis de Gruthuyse, 1472.
Vellum; 285 × 500 mm.

In these letters patent of Edward IV under the Great Seal, 23 Nov. 1472, arms are granted to Louis de Bruges, seigneur de la Gruthuyse, whom Edward had in the previous month with great ceremony created Earl of Winchester. In the middle of the

charter are illuminated the arms: Azure ten mascles or (derived from the Earldom of Winchester), with a canton for England, i.e. Gules a lion passant armed azure. The pen and ink decoration of the ornamental initial 'E' includes a rose and a feather.
Louis de Gruthuyse had acted as host to Edward IV and his brother Richard of Gloucester (afterwards Richard III), with their entourage, during Edward's period of exile in the Low Countries in 1470–71. Edward showed his gratitude by two very distinctive marks of royal favour: the grant of an English earldom and of the 'ensigns worthy of an earl' granted in this patent. The two other best known extant Crown grants of arms in the medieval period are those of Henry VI to his foundations of Eton and King's College, Cambridge.
Bibliography: Archaeologia, xxvi (1834), pp. 265–86 and lvi (1898), pp. 27–38, Pl. III; W. H. St John Hope, *A Grammar of English Heraldry,* 2nd ed., Cambridge, 1953, p. 68; Wagner, 1956, p. 67.
BL Egerton MS. 2830.

39 Rous Roll: English Version,
temp. Richard III.
Vellum; 7·00 × 0·335 m.

An illustrated armorial roll-chronicle
by John Rous, chantry priest of
Guy's Cliffe (Warwicks.), commemorating royal and other
benefactors of Warwick, and
celebrating the deeds of Rous's
patrons, the holders of the Warwick
earldom. Sixty-four figures appear
drawn in pen and ink, beginning
with mythical, royal and historical
persons (including Edward IV and
Richard III), and continuing with
the descent of the Earls of Warwick
to the Beauchamps and Nevilles.
The roll ends with Queen Anne
(Neville), Richard III and their son
Edward shown as Prince of Wales
(created 1483, d. 1484). Each
figure has a biographical notice
beneath and coats of arms painted
on shields or banners above; many
also hold shields and are accompanied by badges and crests. The
text includes blazons of the arms
and mottos (called 'resons'), and
further blazons occur on the dorse
of the roll beneath 94 painted coats
of arms arranged as a continuous
frieze on each margin. Over twenty
genealogical descents inserted
between the figures are thought to
be in Rous's own hand.
The English roll is one of two
versions of the roll-chronicle made
by Rous; the other copy is in Latin,
and has been since 1786 in the
College of Arms. The Latin roll
appears to be the earlier version,
but was altered after the accession
of Henry VII in 1485 to give a more
acceptably Lancastrian flavour.
Bibliography: W. Courthope (ed.),
[*The Rows Roll*], London, 1859;
Aspilogia I, pp. 116–20; C. E.
Wright, 'The Rous Roll: The
English Version', *Brit. Mus Quart.*,
xx (1956), pp. 77–81; Rickert,
1965, pp. 185, 249 n. 11, 11a;
Aspilogia II, pp. 277–78; Wagner,
1972, p. 355; Wright, 1973, pp. 4,
10, 25–26, Pl. III.
BL Additional MS. 48976.

39

40 The Boke of St Albans, 1486.
Paper; 292 × 210 mm.

Printed English treatises of instruction in hawking, hunting, coat armour and the blazoning of arms, produced by the 'Schoolmaster Printer' of St Albans. The former attribution of authorship to Dame Juliana Berners is now refuted. The popularity of this first English sporting and armorial book is attested by its early reprinting (by Wynkyn de Worde, 1496), and by the many reprints and revisions made in the sixteenth and seventeenth centuries. The treatise on the 'Blasyng of Armys' is illustrated with shields in colour which constitute the earliest colour-printed woodcuts in England.
Bibliography: R. Hands, *English Hawking and Hunting in the Boke of St Albans*, Oxford, 1975.
BL G.10547.

41 Grant of Arms and Crest to Thomas and Richard Barowe, 1495.
Vellum; 215 × 528 mm.

Grant, in English, by John Wrythe *al.* Writhe, Garter King of Arms (d. 1504), to Master Thomas Barowe, clerk (Master of the Rolls, 1483), and his brother Richard of Winthorp, Merchant of the Staple, of arms and a crest. The initial letter 'T' encloses an illumination of the arms: Quarterly 1 and 4, Sable two swords in saltire argent between four fleurs-de-lis or, within a bordure compony argent and purpure; 2 and 3, Sable a bar between two fleurs-de-lis or and a roe passant argent; crest, a roe's head argent. Garter's signature is at the foot and his armorial seal appended (a shield of arms charged with a cross between four birds; with helm, mantling, and crest, of a bird crowned). This grant superseded one made to the same grantees by Walter Bellengier, Ireland King of Arms, in 1477 (Add. MS. 37687 C).
Bibliography: W. H. St John Hope, *Proc. Soc. Ants.*, 2nd ser., xvi (1897), pp. 344, 347–48; Wagner, 1967, p. 159, notes 1 and 3.
BL Additional MS. 37687 E.

42 Finger-ring with Shield of Arms, fifteenth century.
Gold; D of hoop 25 mm.

The shield bears two bars and in chief a cinquefoil, possibly the arms of South. 'Black-letter' inscription AL:IS:GOD:WELE inside hoop.
Bibliography: Dalton, 1912, no. 292, Pl. IV; Oman, 1974, p. 104, Pl. 42 B.
BM M&LA Franks Bequest No. 613.

43 Finger-ring with Shield of Arms, late fifteenth century.
Gold; D of hoop 26 mm.

The shield bears two lions passant. 'Black-letter' inscription JE FORT FOY OU JE DAY inside hoop.
Found in the Thames at Battersea.
Bibliography: Dalton, 1912, no. 296, Pl. IV; Oman, 1974, p. 104, Pl. 42A.
BM M&LA Franks Bequest No. 617.

41

II

Banners, Badges and Beasts

Heraldry is 'centred on the shield', but other forms of display have always played their part. In the early period further means for showing arms were provided primarily by the accoutrements of the armed and mounted knight. Indeed, it was the practice of painting arms on the linen surcoat worn over a knight's chainmail (no. 44) which gave rise to the term 'coat of arms'. Arms were also displayed on the saddle-cloth — later the horse-trapper — and on various forms of flag. The claims of the lance-flag are perhaps even greater than those of the shield to have been the earliest form of 'cognizance'. The Bayeux Tapestry contains over thirty examples of lance-flags charged with devices. Such flags also appear prominently on the early equestrian seals (e.g. no. 2).

During the thirteenth and fourteenth centuries there were three principal types of flag in use: the pennon, the banner and the standard. In the absence of surviving examples it is from the evidence of brasses and effigies, from miniatures in illuminated manuscripts, and from other documentary material that our knowledge of their form is derived. The pennon was the flag of the ordinary knight, carried at the top of his lance and pointed or swallow-tailed in shape. It bore the owner's arms or armorial device. The pennons of Sir John d'Aubernoun (no. 19) and Sir Geoffrey Luttrell (no. 23) illustrate how the arms on small triangular pennons were sometimes placed sideways to be upright when the lance was levelled.

Higher-ranking knights banneret and more senior commanders bore their arms upon banners. Early banners were rectangular and attached length-ways along the staff or lance. Good examples of their proportions are pro-vided by the banners of the Hospitallers and Templars in Matthew Paris's marginal drawings (no. 7) and by the Royal banner of Richard II borne by Sir Simon Felbrigge (no. 45). In the fifteenth century banners became virtually square (no. 48), but the modern form of rectangular flag, greater in width than in height, is not found in the Middle Ages.

The third main variety of flag was the standard. Unlike the banner the standard did not bear the arms of the owner but his badge or device. It was a narrow, tapering flag, slit at the end, the length determined by the rank of the bearer. Coloured drawings of standards among the Wriothesley collections (no. 49) illustrate their customary form in the Tudor period when they were particularly popular: an upright panel next to the hoist contains the cross of St George; the rest of the flag is generally parted per fess in two tinctures (frequently the livery colours of the bearer), and is charged with the badge or crest, and with the motto placed in the form of two bends; a number of smaller badges powder the field.

The badges which appear upon standards are the marks or emblems assumed as distinctive devices by a person or family, but displayed alone and not associated with the shield. Much of their significance and the occasions for their use remains obscure. They became fashionable at the court of Edward III and from the fourteenth to the sixteenth century Royal badges are found more frequently than the Royal arms in many forms of decoration, on stone, and in glass, and even make their appearance upon the coinage (no. 179). It is significant that the period of the badge's greatest popularity coincided with an age of civil disorder and the rise of private armies, for among their most important uses was their display on a lord's standard in the field and as a mark of allegiance on the liveries of his retainers. With the increasing elaboration in armorial bearings the advantages of the simpler badge for the purposes of recognition are clear. Perhaps best known of all the badges are those associated with the houses of York and Lancaster; for example, the Yorkist badges of the falcon and fetterlock (nos. 56, 57, 59), the white rose *en soleil* (nos. 58, 59), the boar (nos. 57, 58), the lion of March and the black bull of Clarence (no. 59); and for Lancaster the swan badge (no. 53) and the famous red rose (nos. 58, 68). Many of these badges derived from Royal devices of the fourteenth century. In the sixteenth century began a period of decline in the use of family badges, although in early Tudor times Royal badges and beast-badges on standards continued to flourish.

Figuring prominently among the badges, and also frequently used by the badge's owner for a crest or supporter, are many of the creatures that have come to be regarded as typical heraldic beasts, e.g. the lion, the griffin, the hart and the antelope. Some of the most colourful are to be found in the bestiary (see no. 51), the great compendium of natural history, descended from the Greek *Physiologus*, in which characteristics attributed to real and fabulous animals were combined with elaborate Christian allegorical interpretations. The bestiary was enormously popular as a picture book in the late twelfth and early thirteenth century and clearly had considerable influence on the heraldic imagination. Beasts were commonly adopted as supporters to the shield when these were introduced in the thirteenth century (possibly an invention of the seal engravers' art to decorate the space on the seal between the shield and the legend), and by the end of the fourteenth century at least were not purely ornamental but had gained a heraldic significance. They were also widely used in an architectural context decorating gables or gate-posts and supporting banners or vanes along the roof-line of buildings. The pavilion designed for Henry VIII is a particularly beautiful example of one such series of beasts holding banners (no. 67).

Select Bibliography

De Walden Library, *Banners, Standards and Badges from a Tudor Manuscript in the College of Arms*, London, 1904.
Barnard, F. P., *Edward IV's French Expedition of 1475*, Oxford, 1925.
Stanford London, H., *Royal Beasts*, The Heraldry Society, 1956.

44

44　Miniature of Knight with Lance-flag in the Westminster Psalter, mid-thirteenth century. Vellum; 227 × 157 mm.

A knight, kneeling, holds out his hands as if in homage to the King on the opposite page; the crosses formy on the knight's surcoat appear also on his lance-flag. The picture occurs in a series of five tinted drawings by a mid-thirteenth century artist in the style of Matthew Paris of St Albans. The drawings have been added at the end of the Westminster Psalter (*c*. 1200).
Bibliography: M. R. James, 'The Drawings of Matthew Paris',

Walpole Soc., xiv (1925–6), pp. 24–26, Pl. xxvii; F. Wormald, 'Paintings in Westminster Abbey and Contemporary Paintings', *Proc. Brit. Acad.*, xxxv (1949), pp. 162–64; P. Brieger, *English Art 1216–1307*, Oxford, 1957, pp. 104, 136, 170, 172, 214, Pl. 37b.
BL Royal MS. 2 A. xxii, f. 220.

45　Impression from the Brass of Sir Simon Felbrigge, K.G. (d. 1442), Banner Bearer to King Richard II, 1416.
Paper; 1·72 × 0·52 m.

The figure is in plate-armour with the Garter on his left leg and his right arm supporting the Royal Banner

charged with the attributed arms of Edward the Confessor (no. 203) impaling the Royal arms of England. The copy gives a reversed image of the brass, since the impression is not a 'rubbing', but made by the direct contact of damp paper on the inked brass. One of a series of such impressions made about 1780 by the antiquary Craven Ord (d. 1832). The Craven Ord impressions are the earliest surviving copies of monumental brasses other than freehand drawings.
Bibliography: Stephenson, 1926, p. 333; V. J. Torr, 'A Guide to Craven Ord', *Trans. Mon. Brass Soc.*, ix, pt. ii (1950), pp. 80–91.
BL Additional MS. 32478, f. 40.

46 William Montagu, 1st Earl of Salisbury, in the Salisbury Roll Copy, *temp.* Richard III.
Paper; 379 × 269 mm.

Leaf from the Salisbury roll copy, showing William Montagu, 1st Earl of Salisbury (d. 1344) in full armour with crested helm. He holds a lance with a swallow-tailed pennon charged with a griffin of Montagu. Further pennons with the same device appear in the background.

A contemporary inscription on the drawing refers to William as the founder (in 1337) of Bisham Priory (Berks.), subsequently the family burial place. On the verso of the leaf is a roughly executed coloured drawing of Bisham Priory, represented in the original roll (see description for no. 34) by a very beautiful painting showing considerable architectural detail.
Bibliography: see no. 34.
BL Additional MS. 45133, f. 52***

47 The Streamer of Warwick in the Beauchamp Pageants, after 1483.
Vellum; 279 × 202 mm.

This leaf comes from a series of drawings, each accompanied by an explanatory text in English, illustrating the exploits of Richard Beauchamp, Earl of Warwick, K.G. (1382–1439). The exhibited page (f. 18v.) shows Earl Richard engaged in a sea battle. From the crow's nest of his ship flies his streamer (a form of standard but much greater in length); it bears a cross of St George in the hoist, then the bear and ragged staff badge and a number of smaller ragged staves. A similar 'grete stremour' made for Warwick in 1437 measured forty yards in length and eight yards in breadth. Behind the streamer can be seen the mainsail, emblazoned like a banner with the Earl's arms of Beauchamp quartering Newburgh. The Beauchamp Pageants may have been made for Earl Richard's daughter Anne, Countess of Warwick (d. 1493), who appears prominently in an illustrated genealogy at the end of the fifty-

46

three drawings (ff. 27–28). The purpose of the Pageants was presumably the same as that of the Salisbury and the Rous rolls (nos. 34, 39), namely the glorification of the family. The artist is un-identified but seems likely to have been from the Low Countries, working in England. He may also have worked for John Writhe, Garter King of Arms (1478–1504), for among the Bath ceremony paintings in John Writhe's Garter Book (no. 262) occurs a single drawing which has recently been identified as his work.
Bibliography: William, Earl of Carysfort, *The Pageants of Richard Beauchamp, Earl of Warwick*, Roxburghe Club, 1908; Viscount Dillon, W. H. St John Hope, *Pageant of the Birth, Life and Death of Richard Beauchamp Earl of Warwick K.G. 1381–1439*, London, 1914; Rickert, 1965, p. 250, n. 12; British Museum exhib. cat., *The*

Art of Drawing, 1972, no. 89; NPG., 1973, no. 132, Pls. 1, 2, 4–6; Brussels, Bibliothèque Royale Albert 1er, exhib. cat. *English Illuminated MSS. 700–1500*, 1973, no. 86; Scott, 1976, pp. 55–71.
BL Cotton MS. Julius E. iv, art. 6.

48 Banners in Sir Thomas Wriothesley's Book of Funeral Collections, early sixteenth century. Paper; 335 × 245 mm.

The banner, standard, shield and helm, painted on the left-hand exhibited page (f. 67v.), were those carried at the funeral in 1511 of William Courtenay, Earl of Devon. The paintings accompany a description of the ceremonies by Sir Thomas Wriothesley, Garter King of Arms 1505–34, in a volume of his collections relating to funerals. According to Wriothesley's account, William Courtenay's body was brought by barge from

Greenwich for burial at the Black Friars', London. There in the choir were set small pennons, badges and four banners, each one a 'baneroll of maryage of his blode'. These four funeral banners showing various marshallings of the arms of Courtenay are painted on f. 68. Only a few months earlier Courtenay had been one of the four challengers at the Westminster Tournament (no. 73).
Bibliography: Wright, 1973, p. 25, Pl. 12.
BL Additional MS. 45131.

49 Sir Thomas Wriothesley's Book of Standards, *c.* 1525–54. Paper; 330 × 225 mm.

A volume of coloured drawings of standards, pennons and shields of arms, mostly compiled by Sir Thomas Wriothesley, Garter (1505–34), but with some later additions. On the exhibited pages

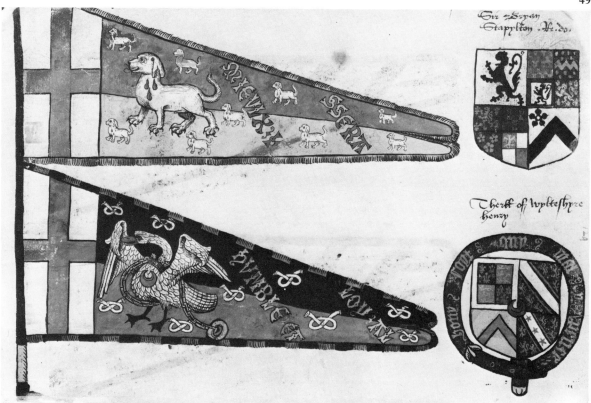

49

(ff. 63v.–64) are standards and shields of Sir Bryan Stapleton (knighted 1504), Henry Stafford, 1st Earl of Wiltshire, (K.G. 1505), Sir Henry Wiloughby (knighted 1489), and Sir Robert Curson (styled 'Lord Curson'). A very similar manuscript collection of standards is in the College of Arms (MS. I.2).

Bibliography: Banners Standards and Badges from a Tudor Manuscript in the College of Arms, De Walden Library, 1904; Wright, 1973, pp. 4, 25, Pl. IV.
BL Additional MS. 45132.

50 Book of London Military Banners, 1648.
Paper; 147 × 90 mm.

This small manuscript contains painted banners of commanders of Parliamentary Horse Troops and Foot Regiments of the City of London in 1642, and of those commanders made since 'the first setleing of the Millitia to this present 1648'. The arms are also given in blazon employing the names of planets for the conventional heraldic colours, e.g. the arms of William Hubert, Captain of a Troop of Horse, are described as 'Quarterly luna and Saturne On a Bend Mars three Lyoncells Passant Sol, Lingued and Armed Jupitur' (f. 22v.).
Lent by Sir Anthony Wagner, Garter Principal King of Arms.

51 Griffin and Elephant in a Bestiary, c. 1200.
Vellum; 307 × 235 mm.

The exhibited miniatures show the Griffin and the Elephant and Castle, both familiar heraldic subjects, in an illuminated Latin bestiary. The manuscript was produced in England during the period when illustrated bestiaries were most popular and an important source for animal subjects in all the arts, including heraldry. The ancient form of griffin is described in the bestiary text: a quadruped with the wings and face of an eagle and all the bodily parts of a lion. The picture, however, gives the creature forelegs with claws. It was this latter

51

form of griffin, half-eagle half-lion, which became so popular in European armoury. The griffin in the picture shows his great strength by holding in his claws a biting horse. The elephant with the war-tower on its back was also a favourite bestiary picture, although it illustrates only a very brief statement in the text: Persians and Indians place wooden towers on elephants and fight from them. In the exhibited miniature the tower's defenders bear shields of arms, but these appear to be purely decorative and not identifiable as heraldic charges.

Bibliography: G. C. Druce, 'The Elephant in Medieval Legend and Art', *Arch. J.*, lxxvi (1919), pp. 1–73; M. R. James, *The Bestiary*, Roxburghe Club, 1928, pp. 15–16; Stanford London, 1956, pp. 17–19; F. McCulloch, *Medieval Latin and French Bestiaries*, N. Carolina, 1960; Rickert, 1965, p. 88; F. Klingender, *Animals in Art and Thought to the end of the Middle Ages*, London 1971, pp. 382–402; Dennys, 1973, pp. 175–79.
BL Harley MS. 4751, ff. 7v–8.

52 Horary Quadrant with Badge of Richard II, 1399
Brass; radius 89 mm.

On the side with the horary quadrant for equal hours is the badge of Richard II (a hart lodged, chained and gorged with a coronet) with this inscription on the encircling band: PRI · 3 · DI · 3 · PASCHA FI. The other side has the 'Tabula bisexti' (i.e. circle of Dominical letters) for twenty-eight years, beginning with 1399.
Bibliography: Guide, 1924, p. 222, Fig. 144.
BM M&LA 60, 5–19, I.

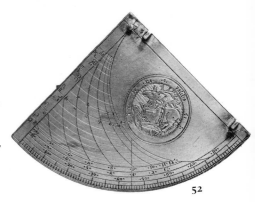

52

55   56

53 The Dunstable Swan Jewel,
early fifteenth century.
Gold with white enamel; H 32 mm.

This is the sole surviving example of
a white enamelled badge in the form
of a chained animal, such as the
white hart worn by Richard II in
the Wilton Diptych (National
Gallery). The swan was a
Lancastrian badge particularly used
by the Princes of Wales in the
fifteenth century. The badge was
used in the fourteenth century by a
number of English noble families
such as the Tonys, de Bohuns,
Beauchamps and Courtenays, who
were proud of their descent from
the Swan Knight of medieval
romance. It was the marriage in
1380 of Mary the younger, co-
heiress of Humphrey de Bohun, to
Henry of Lancaster that brought
the use of the badge into the
House of Lancaster.
Found on the site of the Dominican
Priory at Dunstable (Beds.) in 1965.
Bibliography: J. Cherry, 'The
Dunstable Swan Jewel', *J. Brit.
Arch. Assoc.,* xxxii (1969), pp.
38–53.
BM M&LA 1966, 7–3, 1.

54 Pendant with a Wyvern,
fourteenth or fifteenth century.
Bronze; H 61 mm.

This round pendant was probably
attached to a leather pendant by
the circular stud above. The pendant
is engraved with a wyvern on one
side and arms (Paly of eight
impaling a fleur-de-lis) on the other.
BM M&LA 63, 2–20, 3.

**55 Badge in the Form of a Seated
Talbot,** fifteenth century.
Lead; H 42 mm.

This badge may have belonged to
one of the retainers or supporters
of the Talbot family. The two letters
'ta' beginning the word 'talbot' are
on the dog's collar. The talbot, a
large hunting dog, may have
acquired this name through the
introduction of the breed into
England by the Talbot family in the
fourteenth century. The talbot was
used as a device by the family in the
fifteenth century (no. 242). Political
poems in the mid-fifteenth century
refer to John, Lord Talbot, as
'Talbott, oure goode dogge' and
'Talbott, oure gentille dogge'. The
badge was still in use during the
French expedition of 1513, when

Sir Gilbert Talbot bore on his
standard 'a talbot passant sylver
with a cressent apon his shulder
for a difference'.
Found in Bristol harbour in 1892.
Bibliography: for the use of the
badge see F. P. Barnard, *Edward
IV's French Expedition of 1475,*
Oxford, 1925, pp. 81–82.
BM M&LA 1933, 3–8, 3. (Gift of
L. A. Lawrence)

**56 Badge in the Form of a
Fetterlock Enclosing a Rose,**
fifteenth century.
Lead; H 44 mm.

Both the fetterlock and the rose
are Yorkist badges, though the
fetterlock is usually associated with
the falcon. In a fifteenth-century
memorandum in the Bodleian
Library (Digby MS. 82) which gives
the names of the lordships with the
badges that pertain to the Duke of
York, the badge of the Duchy of
York is given as the falcon and
fetterlock and the badge that the
Duke bears through his lordship
of Clifford Castle is a white rose.
Bibliography: H. Ellis, 'Badges of
the House of York', *Archaeologia,*
xvii (1814), pp. 226–27.
BM M&LA 56, 6–27, 116.

57 Fenn's Book of Badges,
c. 1466–70.
Paper; 285 × 187 mm.

A collection of fifty-seven ink and
wash drawings of badges, mainly of
Yorkist nobles, made about 1466–
70. The drawings were cut out and
laid on sheets in their present form
by the Norfolk antiquary Sir John
Fenn (d. 1794). On the leaf shown
(f. 5) is the falcon and fetterlock
badge for 'the duk of york', and
the boar gorged with a coronet for
'my lorde of glowctr' (Richard
Plantagenet, Duke of Gloucester,
later Richard III). Beneath the boar
badge is the motto: 'tant le
desiere'. Richard III's white boar
probably derives from Edward III's
badge, differenced by a change of
colour.
Bibliography: Aspilogia I, p. 106;
Reading, 1963, no. 11; NPG.,
1973, Pls. 45, 46; Dennys, 1975,
pp. 51, 115, 147.
BL Additional MS. 40742.

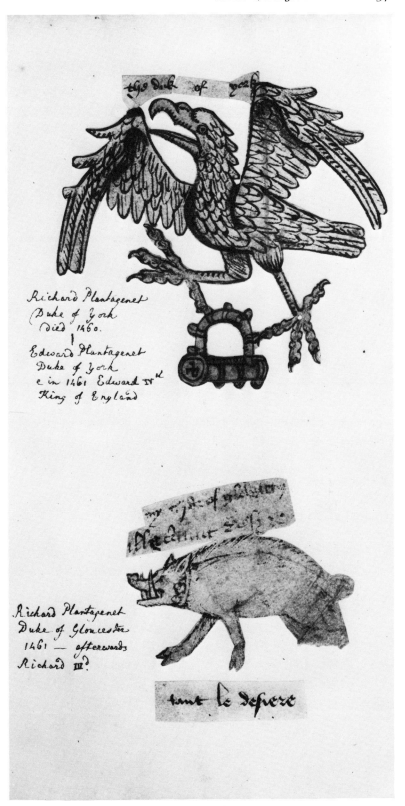

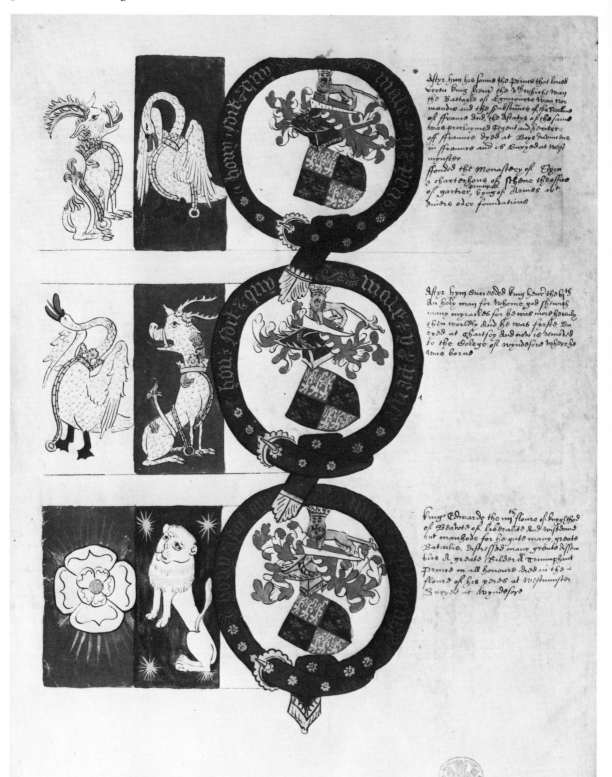

58 Badges, Shields and Crests in Writhe's Garter Armorial (c. 1488), copy c. 1640.
Vellum; 450 × 350 mm.

The manuscript reproduces paintings of badges, shields and crests of Knights of the Garter from John Writhe's Garter Armorial (Part II of no. 262). The badges and arms are arranged by precedence and accompanied by biographical notices. On the exhibited pages (ff. 1v.–2) are displayed on banners the badges of Henry V and Henry VI (antelopes and swans chained and gorged with coronets); Edward IV (a white rose *en soleil* and a lion of March); Richard III (a boar); and Henry VII (a red rose of Lancaster crowned and a dragon). The copy is an example of the Hatton-Dugdale facsimiles of rolls of arms made c. 1640 for Sir Christopher Hatton (d. 1670), under the direction of Sir William Dugdale (see no. 87).
Bibliography: Aspilogia I, pp. xxiii–xxv, 124; Wright, 1973, pp. 6, 25, Pl. 11.
BL Additional MS. 37340.

59 Sir William Segar's Book of Royal Arms and Badges, 1604.
Vellum; 217 × 165 mm.

Dedicated to James I, this manuscript of arms and badges of the Kings of England was written and illuminated by Sir William Segar, Garter (d. 1633). On the exhibited pages (ff. 21v.–22) are the 'Panther Incensed' attributed as a badge to Henry VI, and five badges for Edward IV (the white rose *en soleil*, the falcon in a fetterlock, the sun in splendour, the white lion and the black bull). The heraldic panther was a muddled version of the multi-coloured panther of the bestiary stories who attracts other beasts with its fragrant breath, 'that steameth forth of his nosethrills, and eares like Smoke, which our Paynters mistaking, corruptly doe make fire'.
Sir William Segar, said to have been 'bred up a scrivener', was also the author of several works on chivalry and arms. Recent scholar-

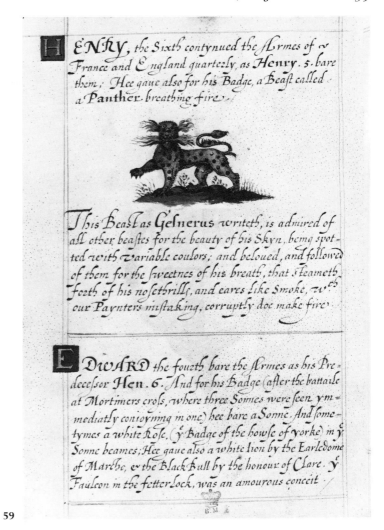

59

ship has given him considerable standing as an artist, attributing to him a group of among the finest Elizabethan portraits. His talents as a practising herald have received less acclaim (no. 82).
Bibliography: E. Auerbach, *Tudor Artists*, London, 1954, pp. 121–22, 185; R. Strong, *The English Icon: Elizabethan & Jacobean Portraiture*, London, 1969, pp. 17–19, 215–24.
BL Harley MS. 6085.

60 Badge in the Form of a Chained Bear and Ragged Staff, fifteenth century.
Lead; H 41 mm (the head of the bear missing).

The bear and the ragged staff were originally two separate devices both used by the Beauchamp family in the latter half of the fourteenth century. It was Richard de Beauchamp, Earl of Warwick (1382–1439), who united the two in a single badge. On his first seal bears appear grasping ragged staves but not chained to them. On his later seals the bears have collars and chains. The badge was also used by Richard Neville, Earl of Warwick, 'the Kingmaker' (1428–71). The badge was probably worn by a retainer.
Bibliography: C. J. Smith, 'The bear and ragged staff', *Amateur Historian*, 3, pt. 5 (1957), pp. 217–19.
BM M&LA 1904, 7–20, 23.

61 A London Binding with Badge of Robert Dudley, Earl of Leicester, *c.* 1560.
Clement of Alexandria, *Opera* [Greek], Florence, 1550.
342 × 224 × 50 mm.

Brown calf, tooled in gold to a panel design with solid and hatched tools and with the bear and ragged staff badge here used by Robert Dudley, Earl of Leicester (d. 1588).
BL G. 11780.

62 Panel with the Arms and Crest of Sir William Belknap, late fifteenth century.
Painting on wood; 489 × 345 mm.

The panel depicts a shield of Sir William Belknap's arms (Quarterly; 1, Sable on a bend cotised argent three eagles displayed; 2, Gules a fess gobony argent and sable between six cross crosslets fitchy or; 3, Bendy of ten or and sable; 4, Or two bends gules) impaling those of his wife, Anne Browne (Argent on a bend cotised sable three water-bougets or). The shield is suspended from a burning beacon with a ducally gorged and chained lizard at the base. Shield, beacon and lizard are set on a foliate diapered red ground. The side frames of the panel are modern.
From Burton Dassett parish church (Warwicks.).
Bibliography: Ward, 'Some Observations on the Antiquity and Use of Beacons', *Archaeologia*, i (3rd ed. 1804), pp. 1–2.
BM M&LA 1922, 5–11, 1.

61

63 Finger-ring with a Lion Passant Reguardant, fifteenth century.
Gold; D of hoop 30 mm.

The bezel bears a lion passant reguardant and a scroll with the 'black-letter' motto NOW : YS : THUS. Found on the site of the battlefield of Towton (1461), this ring has been associated with Henry Percy, 3rd Earl of Northumberland, who died in the battle. However, the Percy arms (see no. 27) do not include a lion passant and there is no evidence to connect the motto with this family.
Bibliography: Dalton, 1912, no. 536, Pl. VII; NPG, 1973, no. 166;

Oman, 1974, pp. 103–104, Pl. 41D.
BM M&LA Franks Bequest No. 771.

64 Finger-ring with Rebus, fifteenth century.
Gold; D of hoop 21 mm.

The rebus engraved on the bezel consists of a cluster of hops and a tun, for Hopton. The inner side of the hoop has the 'black-letter' inscription AMOUR FAIT MOULT ARGENT FAIR TOUT.
Found at Sudbury (Suffolk).
Bibliography: Dalton, 1912, no. 564, Pl. VII; Oman, 1974, p. 102, Pl. 39 D.
BM M&LA Franks Bequest No. 787.

64

65 Finger-ring with Buckle Badge, sixteenth century.
Gold; D of hoop 23 mm.

The buckle is the device of the Pelham family.
Bibliography: Dalton, 1912, no. 482, Pl. VI.
BM M&LA Franks Bequest No. 733.

66 Four Inlaid Tiles from Hailes Abbey with Roses and Portcullises, c. 1525–40.
W 1) 149 mm; 2) 150 mm; 3) 145 mm; 4) 149 mm.

These tiles were first recorded in a floor in the manor house at Southam de la Bere (Glos.) and are identical with tiles found in excavations at Hailes Abbey. The tile series contained the names and rebuses of the last three Abbots of Hailes: Thomas Stafford, Anthony Melton, and Stephen Sagar as well as the Royal arms and badges. The rose and portcullis were commonly used by Henry VII and Henry VIII. The portcullis was a Beaufort badge, and it has also been argued that the portcullis refers to the patronage of the Abbey by Lord Herbert of Raglan, a bastard son of Henry Beaufort, 3rd Duke of Somerset, who in 1509 was granted an indulgence from the Confraternity of Hailes by Abbot Anthony Melton. The initial letter of the indulgence encloses the portcullis of the Beauforts.
Bibliography: Baddeley, 1908, pp. 54, 107, and fig. 25, no. 2; J. Cherry, 'Hailes tiles from Southam de la Bere', *British Museum Yearbook*, 3 (1978) (forthcoming).
BM M&LA tile nos. 1) 13,797; 2) 13,798; 3) 13,806; 4) 13,817.

67 The King's Beasts on a Design for a Royal Pavilion, early sixteenth century.
Paper; 421 × 952 mm.

The crimson and gold pavilion in the design was probably painted in connection with the meeting of Henry VIII of England and Francis I of France at the Field of the Cloth of Gold in the summer of 1520. On the tent-poles are set eighteen 'royal beasts' derived from the badges and supporters of King Henry and his ancestors: four lions, three dragons, six greyhounds, two harts and three heraldic antelopes. The beasts support banners charged with Royal arms or badges, and the tent is further decorated with fleurs-de-lis, Tudor roses, and the royal motto: DIEU ET MON DROIT.
Bibliography: Stanford London, 1956, pp. 7, 56–57.
BL Cotton MS. Augustus iii, f. 18.

Colour plate

68 Roundel with the Red Rose, first half of sixteenth century.
Stained glass; 623 × 293 mm.

The rose has a yellow bud and is surmounted by a yellow crown containing green and red pieces of glass representing jewels. Said to be from Henry VIII's destroyed palace of Nonsuch (Surrey), begun in 1538 (see also no. 216). The red rose is the emblem of the House of Lancaster.
Lent by the Victoria and Albert Museum (Dept. of Ceramics no. C.456–1919).

69 Shield with the Device of the Prince of Wales, 1537–47.
Stained glass; 413 × 356 mm.

The shield bears Party azure and purpure three ostrich feathers argent through a crown or, and scrolls with the motto HIC DEIN. The shield is flanked by the letters EP and is enclosed within a border of Renaissance motifs. The letters represent Prince Edward (later Edward VI), although he was never created Prince of Wales. The Renaissance borderwork and the unusual spelling of the motto suggest that the shield was executed by one of the foreign glaziers working in England in the early sixteenth century.
From Cowick Priory (Devon).
Bibliography: Rackham, 1936, p. 61.
Lent by the Victoria and Albert Museum (Dept. of Ceramics no. C.453–1919).

69

III
The Heralds

The term 'heraldry' has, at least since the fourteenth century, attached itself to armory, the study of coats of arms, but in the wider sense it embraces all the duties of a herald. Heralds became acknowledged experts in the recognition and later the ordering of armorial bearings, but these concerns were not the most important of their early duties and never provided their sole *raison d'être*. The earliest references to heralds of arms occur in French poetry of the twelfth century, and at this date they appear as 'marshals and messengers of the tournament, masters of ceremonies and makers of minstrelsy'. Whether at this time they also had duties in war, as well as in the training for war of the tournament, seems likely but remains unproven. Whatever the case, military and ambassadorial duties certainly did come to occupy an important place in their affairs from the fourteenth to the sixteenth century. From their membership of royal and noble households and their experience in the organising of tournaments arose also an early concern with the conduct of public ceremonies, retained to the present day in the involvement of the heralds in state ceremonial.

Tournaments played an important role in the history of the heralds. It was the growth of the tournament as an elaborate social function which furnished occasions for the most extravagant forms of heraldic display and brought to prominence the heralds with their skills in recognition of arms and in marshalling the ceremonies. This prominence was gained at the expense of the minstrels with whom the heralds were at first closely connected. Perhaps this in some measure explains why the thirteenth-century minstrel, Henri de Laon, bemoaned the increasing professionalism of the tournament and began his satirical poem *Dit des Hérauts* by claiming that for those whose predilections were to be idle and greedy, to talk much while knowing nothing, there could be no better profession than that of the herald; and to be one was his dearest wish.

Just how closely the tournament was the province of the heralds can be seen in manuscript illumination from the Tudor period, a time of spectacular pageantry. The heralds not only perform the task traditionally associated with them of proclaiming the occasion, but are seen assisting the combatants (no. 71), recording arms and keeping the score (no. 72), riding in, and no doubt marshalling, the procession to the lists (no. 74). The only known example of an original tournament challenge (no. 73) seems to have been the product of the heraldic studio of Sir Thomas Wriothesley, Garter, made for the occasion which inspired the greatest of all heraldic pictorial records of the tournament, the Great Tournament Roll of Westminster (no. 74).

Heralds receiving largesse and the ceremonial robes of a Knight of the Bath as their fee at his creation (see cat. no. 262)

Out of the heralds' duties in the tournament arose their need to recognise arms. Before the end of the fourteenth century they were compiling rolls of arms, giving evidence in disputes and becoming very much the acknowledged authorities for the ordering of armorial bearings. In the following century heralds of the royal household came to achieve a monopoly over the granting of arms under the pressure of a steadily increasing demand from the guilds and corporate bodies and from newly wealthy aspirants to respectability. The royal heralds had acted in some measure as a corporate body from the reign of Henry V, but they only obtained their formal incorporation in 1484. Richard III, who as Constable had shared with the Marshal in the supervision of the heralds, granted the charter which made them a body corporate and also conveyed their first home, the great house of Coldharbour (no. 78). At the time of the incorporation John Writhe held the office of Garter (1478–1504). Writhe, and more particularly his son and successor, Sir Thomas Wriothesley, Garter 1505–34 (who augmented his surname 'with the high Sound of three Syllables') were responsible for amassing and preparing an immense corpus of heraldic material. In every section of the exhibition (excluding only the Royal and Personal Arms), Wriothesley's manuscripts can be seen covering all the activities of the heralds and justifying Sir Anthony Wagner's judgement that his work constitutes 'an essential link – if not *the* essential link – between the heraldry of the Middle Ages and heraldry of the College of Arms'.

It is in the records of public ceremonies, state funerals and processions that the heralds are most colourfully depicted; Wriothesley and his fellow heralds appear on the Westminster Tournament Roll (no. 74) in their full apparel. The distinctive dress worn on such occasions was the tabard: a short, wide-sleeved surcoat introduced in about Henry V's time. On the tabards heralds displayed their masters' arms, as for instance Warwick Herald assisting at the tournament in the Beauchamp Pageants (no. 71), and Buckingham and Esperance Pursuivants accompanying the Lords Spiritual in the Parliamentary Processional roll of 1512 (no. 128). From the fifteenth century grants of arms depicted the royal heralds in the initial letter. Thus the Tallow Chandlers' patent (no. 77) has John Smert, Garter (1450–78) with his crown and white rod and wearing a tabard charged with the Royal arms. Pursuivants (originally apprentices to the office of herald) wore their tabards transversely, i.e. with the sleeves at the back and front and the longer parts as sleeves. This practice, known from the fifteenth century and continuing until the late seventeenth century, can be seen on the Tournament Roll, and the pursuivant in Sir Peter Lely's Garter ceremony drawings (no. 92) is also clad in this way. The earliest surviving English tabard is that of Sir William Dugdale, d. 1686 (no. 88), bearing the Stuart Royal arms. It is only from the following century that there survives a full set of a King of Arms' insignia, i.e. sceptre, crown and badge (nos. 101–103).

An important part of the heralds' activities in the post-medieval period was antiquarian and genealogical. The system of Visitations employed in England between *circa* 1530 and 1686, whereby the Kings of Arms or their deputies carried out heraldic surveys in order to regulate the use of arms, led to the recording of genealogies, charters, seals and evidences from monuments and stained glass. The impetus to antiquarian and genealogical

The Court Room of the College of Arms during a session of the Court of Chivalry in the eighteenth century (aquatint by J. Bluck after Pugin and Rowlandson's engraving)

studies was further strengthened by the Elizabethan fashion for elaborate pedigrees which the heralds sought to provide. While scholarly attention has tended to denigrate the heralds' genealogical skills it should nonetheless be remembered that it was owing to the copying and collecting instincts of men like Sir Thomas Wriothesley, the Elizabethan scholar Robert Glover, Somerset (1577–88), Nicholas Charles (no. 83) and the great William Camden (no. 81) that much historical evidence has survived. This is reflected in the number of rolls of arms bearing the names of heralds as later owners and copyists (e.g. nos. 12, 24). It may be that the value of the heralds' antiquarian collections as records of now lost monumental art has not yet been sufficiently appreciated. The great Book of Draughts or Monuments (no. 87) undertaken by Sir William Dugdale and his servant William Sedgwick on the eve of the Civil War is a notable example, but one among many in a tradition of painstaking antiquarian researches which began even before the Reformation. If some heralds could be credulous, and even fraudulent, in furthering tenuous claims to a distinguished ancestry, against this can be set the work of many others which remains as a lasting contribution to historical scholarship.

Select Bibliography

Wagner, A. R., *Heralds and Heraldry in the Middle Ages*, 2nd ed., Oxford, 1956.
Godfrey, W. H., Wagner, A. R., Stanford London, H., *The College of Arms*, London Survey Committee, 1963.
Wagner, A. R., *Heralds of England*, London, 1967.

70 The Military Roll of Arms,
before 1448.
Paper; 339 × 288 m.

Part of a series of coloured drawings of pairs of jousting knights, armed alternately with lances and swords, their shields, tabards and horse trappers displaying their arms. The exhibited pages (ff. 36v.–37) occur among thirty-one leaves of the roll (ff. 9–40v.) in a volume of miscellaneous heraldic material known after one of its earliest owners as 'Sir Thomas Holme's Book' (Sir Thomas was Clarenceux King of Arms 1476–94). Further leaves are in a volume of Sir Thomas Wriothesley's collections (Add. MS. 45133; see nos. 34, 46). The Military Roll is partially arranged by counties, and the lively equestrian figures are uniform throughout, acting not as 'portraits' but as models for the display of arms. The manuscript therefore forms a Local roll of arms in pictorial form, possibly compiled as a heraldic Visitation record. The volume has been identified as the 'book of Visitation of many Shires . . . painted with men of armes' made by Roger Legh, Clarenceux King of Arms 1435–60.
Bibliography: Aspilogia I, pp. 92–94; Wagner, 1956, pp. 111–13, 150; *Aspilogia* II, pp. 271–73.
BL Harley MS. 4205.

Colour plate

71 A Tournament in the Beauchamp Pageants, after 1483.
Vellum; 278 × 204 mm.

71

In this drawing from the series of Beauchamp Pageants (see no. 47) Richard Beauchamp, Earl of Warwick (d. 1439), is shown jousting at Guines in 1414 before the French king. Warwick Herald, in a tabard of his master's arms, stands behind the jousters holding two saddles. In the stand to the right of the French king are three further heralds (or perhaps princes), one in a tabard of the Royal arms of England, and two displaying the arms of France.
Bibliography: see no. 47; Wagner, 1967, Pl. IX.
BL Cotton MS. Julius E. iv, art. 6, f. 15v.

72 Armorial Jousting-cheque for the Field of the Cloth of Gold, 1520.
Vellum; 365 × 273 mm.

The first page of a roll of arms for those taking part in a joust at the Field of the Cloth of Gold; at the top are the Royal arms of King Francis I of France within a collar of the Order of St Michael, and the Royal arms of King Henry VIII of England within a collar of the Order of the Garter. The margins to the left of the Royal arms have been used to score one of the jousts.
Bibliography: O. Barron, 'Heraldry', *Enc. Brit.* (11th ed.), Pl. IV; Ffoulkes, 1912, pp. 46–47, Pl. IX; BHA., p. 63; Dennys, 1975, p. 33 and plate opposite.
Lent by the Society of Antiquaries of London (MS. 136, part 2, f. 1).

73 Challenge for the Westminster Tournament, 1511.
Vellum; 460 × 354 mm.

This letter of challenge is for jousts to be held in honour of the birth of a Prince. The jousts were those celebrated in the Great Tournament Roll of Westminster (no. 74). An allegorical theme for the tournament is stated in the letter of challenge; Queen *Noble renome*, who has heard of the birth of a Prince in England and of the great rejoicing, is sending four knights born in her realm of *Ceure Noble* to accomplish feats of arms. The four knights are named *Ceure loyall* (the role played by Henry VIII), *Vailliaunt desyre* (Sir

Thomas Knyvet), *Bone voloyr* (Sir William Courtenay), and *Joyous panser* (Sir Edward Neville; given as *Joyeulx Penser* on the Tournament Roll). Following the allegorical preamble are articles of combat for the joust. In the margin of the letter is painted a tree ornamented with roses and pomegranates and hung with shields of the Challengers: at the top the King's shield, Azure and gules quarterly, bears a device for 'Ceure Loyall', a golden heart joined to a gold letter 'L' by a cord and tassel; the other three shields, all azure, bear the monograms of the challengers' assumed names. At the foot of the articles of combat are the signatures of King Henry and of the combatants or 'Answerers' for each of the two days of the Tournament. The responsibility for issuing the challenge would have belonged to the heralds. As the reverse of the document bears the 'Ihc' monogram which is a feature of many of the MSS. of Sir Thomas Wriothesley, Garter, the challenge, like the Great Tournament Roll, may well have been the product of his workshop.
Bibliography: H. Ellis, *Original Letters Illustrative of English History*, 2nd series, i, London, 1827, pp. 179–87; Ffoulkes, 1912, pp. 36–37, Pl. V; S. Anglo, 'Financial and Heraldic Records of the English Tournament', *J. Soc. Archivists*, ii, no. 5 (1962), p. 187; Anglo, 1968, i, pp. 28–29, 51–53, 74, 91 and App. I, part II.
BL Harley Charter 83 H 1.

74 The Great Tournament Roll of Westminster, 1511.
Vellum; 0·37 × 17·85 m.

72

Illuminated roll recording the tournament held at Westminster on 12 and 13 February 1510/1511 by Henry VIII, to celebrate the birth to Katherine of Aragon of a son, Henry Duke of Cornwall (b. 1 Jan., d. 22 Feb. 1510/1511). The roll, here exhibited at full length for the first time, depicts three scenes from the Tournament: the entry procession to the lists on the second day of the jousts (membranes 2–23); a view of the King tilting, watched by the Queen with members of the court from an elaborate tilt gallery (membranes 24–27); and finally the procession returning from the lists (membranes 28–35).
Both style and subject matter suggest a heraldic authorship, and the Tournament Roll was almost certainly prepared in the studio of Sir Thomas Wriothesley, Garter King of Arms. The roll has always, as far as is known, remained in the possession of the heralds, and appeared in the first catalogue of the College of Arms in 1618.
Bibliography: Ffoulkes 1912, pp. 34–42, Pl. VIII; HCEC., no. 23, Pls. VI–IX (lists earlier exhibitions); Anglo, 1968.
Lent by the College of Arms.

Colour plate

75 Horse Trapping with Shield, fourteenth or fifteenth century.
Bronze; H 70 mm.

This trapping, which was probably attached to the top of the horse's headstall, is in three parts. The bottom part has rectangular openings and rivet holes for straps, the central section has one arm and holes for three others from which heraldic pendants may have hung, and the topmost part ends in a shield bearing four lozenges gules between three cinquefoils 2 and 1.
BM M&LA OA 242.

76 Coloured Rubbing of Brass of Sir Hugh Hastings (d. 1347).
2·3 × 0·98 m.

The figure wears a rounded bascinet and a mixture of chainmail and

plate-armour with a surcoat. On the surcoat and the heater-shaped shield are the Hastings arms, a maunch (delicately diapered) differenced by a label of three points overall; these were originally enamelled. The figure of Hastings is set within an elaborate canopy and side-shafts, the latter containing small figures in armour of (l) Edward III, Thomas Beauchamp Earl of Warwick, (r) Henry Earl of Lancaster, Ralph Lord Stafford, Almeric Lord St Amand. In the canopy gable is St George and the dragon and above, in two niches, is the Coronation of the Virgin. When Addington made this rubbing from the original brass in Elsing church (Norfolk), a considerable amount of it was already missing. A more complete version is known from the Craven Ord collection in the Dept. of MSS.

This brass was used as evidence in the famous Grey *versus* Hastings case in the Court of Chivalry. On 6 August 1408, the defendant, Sir Edward Hastings, had the proceedings adjourned from Norwich to Elsing so that he could cite before the Court the heraldry on his great-grandfather's brass and in the church windows. A detailed description of the monument was made on this occasion.
Bibliography: Druitt, 1906, pp. 154–56; Macklin, 1913, pp. 47–50; Stephenson, 1926, pp. 331–32; A. R. Wagner and J. G. Mann, 'A Fifteenth-century Description of the Brass of Sir Hugh Hastings at Elsing, Norfolk', *Antiq. J.*, xix (1939), pp. 421–28; H. K. Cameron, 'Monumental Brasses at Gerald Kerin Ltd', *Trans. Mon. Brass Soc.*, x (1963–68), pp. 202–203.
BL Additional MS. 32490 B (12).

Colour plate

77 Grant of Arms by John Smert, Garter King of Arms, to the Worshipful Company of Tallow Chandlers, 1456.
Vellum; 280 × 400 mm.

Grant in French by Smert, who is depicted in the initial wearing his

tabard and crown. He points with his rod to the Company arms (on a field of six pieces azure and argent three doves argent membered gules, each holding in its beak an olive branch or), crest and mantling displayed in the left border. Attached to the grant is a red wax seal bearing Smert's arms. The decoration of the grant has been attributed to the artist William Abell.
John Smert was the second holder of the office of Garter King of Arms, succeeding his father-in-law William Bruges (see no. 237) in 1450; he remained Garter until his death in 1478.
Bibliography: Bromley and Child, 1960, pp. 237–39, Pl. 50; Wagner, 1967, Pl. VIII; Alexander, 1972, p. 167; R. Monier-Williams, *The Tallow Chandlers of London*, iii, London, 1973, pp. 40–43, col. frontispiece.
Lent by the Court of the Worshipful Company of Tallow Chandlers.

78 Richard III's Charter of Incorporation and Grant of a House to the Heralds, 1484.
Vellum; 340 × 514 mm.

By these letters patent of 2 March 1483/4, Richard III constituted the heralds and pursuivants, with their successors in office, a body corporate with perpetual succession and a common seal. This is the first formal charter of incorporation for the heralds.
Included in the charter is the conveyance of a great house in the City of London called 'Coldharbour' for the use of the twelve principal heralds. The heralds' enjoyment of Coldharbour was to be short-lived, for Richard's successor Henry VII recovered the house in 1487, and gave it to his mother, Lady Margaret Beaufort, for life. Whether Henry by his Act of Resumption in 1485 also cancelled the grant of incorporation is not clear. Certainly the heralds obtained a new charter of incorporation from Philip and Mary in 1555, together with the grant of a house called Derby Place as a new home. The present College of Arms was built on the site of the old Derby House which was burnt

down in the Great Fire of 1666.
Bibliography: CA., pp. 1–2; Wagner, 1967, pp. 123, 130, 134–35. BL Cotton MS. Faustina E. i, ff. 30v.–31.

79 Plaque of Thomas Tonge, Clarenceux King of Arms, 1554.
Copper-gilt and enamelled; 172 × 133 mm.

The plaque bears a shield of Tonge's arms (Azure a bend cotised between six martlets or) impaling those of his wife (Or a chevron gules between three popinjays vert armed and langued gules within a bordure azure bezanty), enclosed within a wreath. Above is the motto ESPOER · EN · DIEV · At the base is this inscription: THE · ARMYS · OF · THE · RYGTH · WORSHEPFVL · MAISTER · TONGE · OTHERWYSSE · CALLYD · MAISTER · CLARENCIVS · AND · MESTERIS · SVSAN · HYS · WYFE · 1554.
Thomas Tonge, having been Norroy King of Arms since 1522, filled the office of Clarenceux from 1534 until his death two years later. His wife Susan (née White), who survived him by nearly thirty years, was First Lady of the Privy Chamber to Queen Mary. The plaque must have been commissioned by her.
Bibliography: SAHE., no. 93, Pl. XII; CA., p. 82.
Lent by the Victoria and Albert Museum (Dept. of Metalwork no. 4358–85).

80 The Funeral Procession (1603) of Queen Elizabeth I, early seventeenth century.
Paper; (1) 255 × 745 mm; (2) 255 × 740 mm.

Two leaves from a series of paintings of Elizabeth's funeral procession. (1) Heralds in the procession wearing robes of mourning with hoods and tabards (f. 36v.). Somerset and Richmond Heralds are shown following the royal banner borne by the Earl of Pembroke assisted by Lord Howard of Effingham. Next follow York and Chester Heralds bearing the helm, crest, and target, and two Kings of

81

Arms, William Segar, Norroy (see nos. 59, 82), with the sword, and William Camden, Clarenceux (see no. 81), holding up a tabard of the Royal arms.

(2) The chariot with the coffin drawn by four horses (f. 37v.). The Queen's effigy lies on a coffin covered in purple velvet. A canopy is borne over her by six knights, and twelve noblemen surround the chariot bearing banners with the arms of the Queen's royal ancestors impaling the arms of their wives. A pen and ink copy of the processional drawings, in roll form (Add. MS. 5408), has been attributed to William Camden, but does not appear to be in his hand.

Bibliography: Vetusta Monumenta, iii, 1791, Pls. XVIII–XXIV (from Add. MS. 5408).

BL Additional MS. 35324, ff. 26–39.

Colour plate

81 Portrait of William Camden (d. 1623), Clarenceux King of Arms, seventeenth century.
Oil on canvas; 1·915 × 1·052 m.

Camden is depicted in three-quarters length, wearing his tabard and with his right hand resting on his book *Britannia*. On the plinth below is this text:

> GULIELMUS CAMDENUS
> Clarentius,
> PATRE Peniculario oriundus;
> ambo
> Hujusce Communitatis
> Socij egregij

The portrait, which has been attributed to Daniel Mytens the Elder (1590–1648), was presented to the Painter-Stainers' Company by Sylvanus Morgan, Master in 1676. Camden was the son of a painter-stainer and was himself a liveryman of the Company. He became Clarenceux in 1597, and held the office until his death. One of the founders of the Elizabethan Society of Antiquaries, he was amongst the best antiquarians and topographers of all the heralds.

Bibliography: HCEC., no. 6, Pl. XVI. Lent by the Court of the Worshipful Company of Painter-Stainers.

82

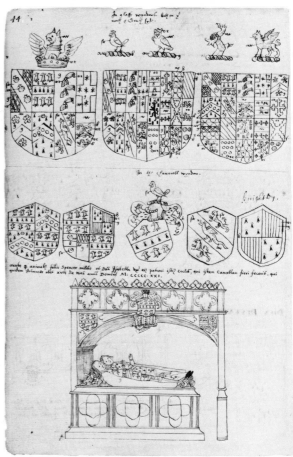

83

82 Engraving of Sir William Segar (d. 1633), Garter King of Arms, early seventeenth century.
181 × 111 mm.

Half-length portrait in an elaborate oval cartouche depicting Segar wearing the Garter mantle and a pendant with the arms of his office, and carrying his sceptre of office. Above his head are his personal arms (Quarterly, 1 and 4, a cross moline, 2 and 3, a chevron between three mullets) and crest. Engraved by Francis Delaram (1590–1627). Segar was nominated Garter in 1604 but the appointment only became effective in 1607. Not over-scrupulous in compiling family pedigrees, he was briefly in-carcerated in the Marshalsea Prison for selling arms (Aragon with a canton for Brabant) to the public hangman (see also no. 59).

Bibliography: British Portraits Cat., iv, p. 51.
BM P&D 1862–10–11–232.

83 Church Notes by Nicholas Charles, early seventeenth century.
Paper; 297 × 200 mm.

Volume containing notes by Nicholas Charles, Lancaster Herald, (1609–13), Richard St George, Clarenceux (1625–35), and later writers, on church monuments and glass in the City of London and many counties. On ff. 70v. and 71 are drawings by Charles of shields of arms in trick and sepulchral monuments in Great Brington church (Northants.). They include the still surviving tombs of Sir John Spencer (d. 1522) and Sir John Spencer (d. 1586); the latter monument was made by Jasper Hollemans of Burton-on-Trent.

Some of the shields of arms still exist in the glass, but not the inscription given on f. 70v. which states that the chancel was built by the first John Spencer.
BL Lansdowne MS. 874.

84 Drawings of Monuments in Henry Lilly's Genealogy of the Earl of Portland, 1632.
Vellum; 405 × 280 mm.

The exhibited drawings (ff. 114v.–115) appear in a volume containing an elaborate genealogy of the Weston and Cave families illustrated with arms in colour, copies of charters and seals and other evidences, compiled for Richard Weston, 'ex industria et labore Hen. Lily Rouge-rose'. The genealogy is certified by Sir William Segar, Garter (see nos. 59, 82), and confirmed by his seal in a silver box.

The silver-gilt clasps on the original blue velvet binding bear the arms of the 1st and 2nd Earls of Portland impaling those of their wives. Henry Lilly *al.* Lily (d. 1638), created Rose Rouge Pursuivant in 1634, and Rouge Dragon Pursuivant in 1638, was a prolific genealogist and a herald painter. A similar volume of lavishly illuminated genealogy compiled by him for the Howard Dukes of Norfolk is at Arundel Castle. Lilly's servant William Sedgwick, arms painter, may have assisted him with these two volumes which include drawings very similar in style to Sedgwick's work on the Book of Monuments for Sir William Dugdale (no. 87). The exhibited pages show wall monuments of the Weston family in Rugeley church (Staffs.), which are no longer extant.
Bibliography: CA., pp. 221–22; C. E. Wright, *Fontes Harleiani*, London, 1972, p. 224.
BL Additional MS. 18667.

85 Cup of Henry Lilly, Rouge Dragon Pursuivant, 1638.
Silver; hall-marked London, 1638; H 222 mm, D 120 mm.

The bowl of the cup bears Lilly's arms (three lilies within a bordure), and the inscription: EX DONO HENRICI LILLY: ROUGE DRAGON: Lilly was a liveryman of the Painter-Stainers' Company, to whom he presented the cup. See also no. 84.
Bibliography: W. A. D. Englefield, *The History of the Painter-Stainers Company of London*, London, 1923, p. iv, pl. opp. p. 112.
Lent by the Court of the Worshipful Company of Painter-Stainers.

86 Portrait of Sir William Dugdale (d. 1686), Garter King of Arms, 1677–86.
Oil on canvas; 978 × 854 mm.

This head and shoulders portrait shows Dugdale wearing his badge of office. Sir William Dugdale was one of the foremost English scholars of the seventeenth century (see no. 87); amongst his most important published works are the *Monasticon Anglicanum* and *The Baronage of*

England. Prior to his becoming Garter in 1677, he had been Norroy King of Arms, from which period dates another portrait, painted by the Dutch artist Pieter Borsseler.
Bibliography: Dugdale, 1953, p. 88.
Lent by Sir William Dugdale, Bt.

87 Sir William Dugdale's Book of Monuments, 1640–41.
Paper; 425 × 280 mm.

In the summers of 1640 and 1641, Sir William Dugdale, foreseeing the 'near approaching storm', took with him an illustrator named William Sedgwick (also employed by Sir Christopher Hatton and Henry Lilly, see no. 84) on a tour in London and the Midlands to record monuments and stained glass 'to the end that the memory of them, in case of that destruction, then imminent, might be preserved for future and better times'. The tombs depicted on the exhibited pages are from Lichfield Cathedral. On f. 4v is the effigy of a knight lying on a tomb chest with shields of arms in cusped niches; the figure can be identified from the heraldry as Ralph, 3rd Lord Basset of Drayton (d. 1390). On f. 5 is an elaborate monument containing within niches the kneeling figures of Robert

Master, chancellor of Coventry and Lichfield diocese (d. 1625) and his wife Catherine. Dugdale's fears were well-justified at Lichfield, for both tombs were destroyed during the sack of the Cathedral by the Parliamentary army in 1643.
Bibliography: W. Hamper (ed.), *The Life, diary and correspondence of Sir W[illiam] D[ugdale]*, London, 1827, p. 14; SAHE., no. 187; Dugdale, 1953, p. 84; Stanford London, 1970, App. XVIII, Pls. XIV, XV.
BL Loan MS. 38 (on loan from the Trustees of the Winchilsea Settled Estates).

88 Tabard of Sir William Dugdale, Garter King of Arms, 1677–86.
0.849 × 1.545 m (arms outstretched).

Red and blue velvet with applied heraldic decoration in cloth of gold and linen, embroidered with silver-gilt and thread, twist, bullion and purl in laid and couched work. The front, back and arms bear the Royal arms as used between 1603 and 1688. This is the oldest surviving English herald's tabard.
Bibliography: SAHE., no. 97, Pl. XIII; HCEC., no. 70, Pl. XVIII.
Lent by Sir William Dugdale, Bt.
Colour plate

87

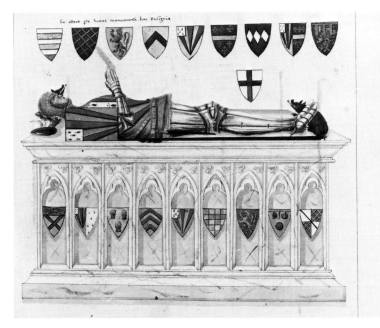

91

Sir John Dugdale, son of Sir William (see nos. 86–88). John became Norroy King of Arms in 1686 and died in 1700.
Bibliography: SAHE., no. 98.
Lent by Sir William Dugdale, Bt.

91 Portrait of Elias Ashmole (d. 1692), Windsor Herald, *c.* 1660–75.
Oil on canvas; 1·592 × 1·285 m.

Ashmole is depicted in three-quarter length, wearing his tabard and collar of ss. In his right hand he holds a charter with a large seal attached. In the background is Windsor Castle. A fervent Royalist, Elias Ashmole was created Windsor Herald at the Restoration in 1660 and resigned in 1675. The founder of the Ashmolean Museum and a noted antiquarian, his most famous work is *The Institution, Laws and Ceremonies of the Most Noble Order of the Garter,* published in 1672. Ashmole's wife Elizabeth was the daughter of Sir William Dugdale, Garter (see nos. 86–88).
Bibliography: Wagner, 1967, Pl. XXIII.
Lent by Sir William Dugdale, Bt.

92 Drawings of Two Heralds and a Pursuivant by Sir Peter Lely, 1663–71.
Black oiled chalk, heightened with white, on blue-grey paper;
(1) 518 × 363 mm; (2) 495 × 251 mm.

(1) Two heralds in their tabards, engaged in conversation; the figure on the left is unfinished. A tentative identification of one as Henry Dethick, Richmond Herald (1677–1704), cannot be proven.
(2) A pursuivant, with his tabard worn in the customary transverse position (see p. 44).
These two drawings form part of an extensive series now dispersed amongst many collections (see also no. 241), illustrating the ceremonies of the Order of the Garter on St George's Day. The identification of certain of the figures points to a dating of the drawings to between 1663 and 1671. The precise purpose for which they were intended has not been firmly established; possibly they were connected with a project

89 Herald's Collar, seventeenth–eighteenth century (?)
Silver, parcel-gilt, with unidentified maker's mark; L 1·962 m.

The collar consists of a chain of ss. Suspended on the front and reverse are two badges, each consisting of a galloping horse, a rose and a thistle surmounted by the crown of Charlemagne and a royal crown, with the motto DIEU MON DROIT below. The collar is traditionally considered to have belonged to Sir William Dugdale (d. 1686), but the badges do not represent his office of Garter; instead they are composed of elements of the Hanoverian arms. Consequently they must date from between 1714 and 1837, when the arms of Hanover are quartered in

the Royal shield. The only member of the Dugdale family who was a herald in this period was John, Mowbray Herald between 1713 and 1749 (see nos. 96, 97). Possibly the collar does date from Sir William's time, in which case the badges were added subsequently, replacing the original Garter badge.
Lent by Sir William Dugdale, Bt.

90 Tabard of Sir John Dugdale, Norroy King of Arms, late seventeenth century.
Satin (for the embroidery technique see no. 88); 0·864 × 1·474 m (arms outstretched).

The front, back and arms bear the Royal arms as used between 1603 and 1688. This tabard belonged to

for mural decoration. The artist, Sir Peter Lely (1618–80), became Principal Painter to King Charles II in 1661 and was the leading portrait painter of his time in England.
Bibliography: Croft-Murray and Hulton, 1960, pp. 409–16; Wagner, 1967, Pls. XXV, XXIX.
Lent by the Courtauld Institute of Art (1), and the Victoria and Albert Museum (Dept. of Prints and Drawings and Paintings no. PD. 140) (2).

93 Hampshire Seals collected on Heraldic Visitation, 1686.
Red wax on paper; 187 × 147 mm.

Impressions of the seals of towns and families in Hampshire and the Isle of Wight, collected in July and August 1686 by Robert Dale (Richmond Herald 1721), during the heraldic Visitation at which he assisted as clerk to Sir Henry St George the Younger, Clarenceux. The itinerary of the Visitation is revealed from Dale's notes on each seal. Commissions for heraldic Visitations ceased with the Revolution of 1688, denying heralds such opportunities for taking the initiative in securing records.
Bibliography: Wagner, 1952, pp. 40, 76; CA., p. 148.
BL Additional MS. 43872.

94 Engraving of Peter Le Neve (d. 1729), Norroy King of Arms, 1773.
135 × 115 mm.

Half-length portrait in an oval frame showing Le Neve in a tabard with a collar of ss and a pendant bearing the arms of his office. This engraving by John Ogborne after Vertue's portrait was published by J. Thane. Le Neve, who became Norroy in 1704, was a noted antiquarian and book collector. He was described by another herald as '. . . of a sordid, selfish disposition . . . cared for nobody, nor did anyone value him . . .'.
Bibliography: British Portraits Cat., iii, p. 48.
BM P&D 1892–12–1–91.

95 Seal Matrix of Peter Le Neve, Norroy King of Arms, 1704.
Silver; D 55 mm.

Engraved with the arms of the office of Norroy (a cross and in chief a lion passant guardant crowned between a fleur-de-lis on the dexter and a key on the sinister) impaling Le Neve (on a cross five fleurs-de-lis, in dexter chief a crescent). Legend: SIGILL: PETRI LE: NEVE ARMIG: NORROY REGIS ARMORUM.
Bibliography: Tonnochy 1952, no. 458.
BM M&LA 50, 9–24, 6. (Gift of Lady Fellows)

95

96

96 Engraved Armorial Bookplate of John Dugdale, Mowbray Herald, 1729.
119 × 88 mm.

Below the shield and motto is the legend NICHOLLS SCULP: 1729. The bookplate was probably that of John Dugdale, Mowbray Herald between 1713 and 1749. It provided the design for the shield of arms on no. 97.
Bibliography: Book Plates Cat., i, no. 9235, p. 322.
BM P&D Bookplates no. 9235.

97 Caddy Tray with the Arms of Dugdale, c. 1745.
Porcelain, decorated in enamels; L 124 mm.

The arms (Azure a cross moline or in dexter chief a roundel), crest and motto PESTIS PATRIAE PIGRITIES, are copied from the Dugdale family bookplate (no. 96), but the tinctures are incorrect. The tray belongs to a service made in China during the reign of the Ch'ien-lung emperor (1736–95), Ch'ing dynasty, probably for John Dugdale, Mowbray Herald Extraordinary (d. 1749); he was Sir William's great-grandson (see nos. 86–88).
Bibliography: Howard, 1974, p. 441.
BM OA 1887, 12–18, 25 (Franks 913+). (Revd C. H. Walker Bequest)

98 Engraving of John Anstis the Elder (d. 1744), Garter King of Arms, 1803.
146 × 114 mm.

Half-length portrait showing Anstis wearing a tabard (see no. 100), collar of ss and a pendant badge of the Order of the Bath. Engraved by Thomas Milton after the portrait by Thomas Maynard and published by Debrett and Egerton. Amongst the most scholarly of the heralds, Anstis only became Garter in 1719 after much opposition. He was the prime mover behind the institution of the Order of the Bath in 1725.
Bibliography: British Portraits Cat.,
vi, p. 14.
BM P&D 1920–12–11–138.

99 'Aspilogia', A Treatise on Seals by John Anstis the Elder, Garter King of Arms, eighteenth century.
Paper; 354 × 225 mm.

'*Aspilogia, sive de Iconibus scutariis Gentilitiis commentarius*', an unpublished discourse in two volumes on heraldic seals by John Anstis the Elder, Garter (Stowe MSS. 665, 666). The second volume of Anstis' unfinished treatise includes many facsimiles and copies of charters with the seals carefully drawn. The exhibited pages (ff. 34v.–35) show seals and charters from the collections of Anstis' fellow herald and antiquary Peter Le Neve, Norroy (see nos. 94, 95). Anstis borrowed the title 'Aspilogia' from the antiquary Sir Henry Spelman (d. 1641), whose treatise on heraldry was published under this title. The tradition continues with the adoption of the name for the series of volumes devoted to the materials of heraldry published by the Society of Antiquaries and the Harleian Society.
Bibliography: CA., pp. 56–57.
Wright, 1973, p. 18.
BL Stowe MS. 666.

100 Tabard of John Anstis, Garter King of Arms, eighteenth century.
0·889 × 1·448 m (arms outstretched).

Red and blue velvet with applied heraldic decoration in cloth of gold

98 △   ▽ 99

and linen, embroidered with silver-gilt and silver thread, twist, bullion and purl in laid and couched work. Some raised work and additional decoration with spangles, black beads and embroidery. The front, back and arms bear the Royal arms as used between 1714 and 1801. The tabard is probably that of John Anstis the Elder (see no. 98), or possibly that of his son John; from 1727 until the elder Anstis' death in 1744 they held the office of Garter jointly. John the Younger was sole Garter King of Arms from 1744 until his own death in 1754; of his abilities as a herald it was said that he was 'only remarkable for knowing nothing whatever of the matter'.

Bibliography: Reading, 1963, no. 211; Windsor, 1975, no. 107.
Lent by the Victoria and Albert Museum (Dept. of Textiles no. T.1–1937).

101 Badge and Chain of Office of John Anstis the Elder, Garter King of Arms (1719–44), *c.* 1719.
Gold and enamelled; 70 × 35 mm (badge only).

The chain has 250 oval, three 8-shaped and one circular links. The gold badge is enamelled on the front and back with St George's cross impaling the Royal arms as used between 1714 and 1801, enclosed by the Garter and motto and surmounted by a crown. In common with his sceptre (no. 102), the badge and chain are shown in a portrait of Anstis in the College of Arms. This particular badge has been used by Garter King of Arms since 1645.

Bibliography: Wagner, 1967, p. 88; Windsor, 1975, nos. 109, 110.
Lent by the Victoria and Albert Museum (Dept. of Metalwork nos. M.5–1937, M.6–1937).

102 Sceptre of John Anstis the Elder, Garter King of Arms (1719–44), *c.* 1719.
Silver, parcel-gilt, the head of enamelled gold; maker's mark of Francis Garthorne; L 610 mm.

The shaft is parcel-gilt, terminating in a wooden grip and a spherical pommel with cut-card work. The head is enamelled on two sides with St George's cross impaling the Royal arms as used between 1714 and 1801; the smaller sides have the cross of St George within the Garter. On the top is a crown. The maker, Francis Garthorne, was active in London between at least 1697 and 1726. The sceptre is depicted in a portrait of Anstis in the College of Arms. Since his time the shaft on heralds' sceptres has been of gold, not silver.

Bibliography: Windsor, 1975, no. 111.
Lent by the Victoria and Albert Museum (Dept. of Metalwork no. M.9–1937).

103 Crown of John Anstis the Elder, Garter King of Arms (1719–44), *c.* 1719.
Silver-gilt; D 210 mm.

The crown has leaf ornament and a cable-moulded rim. The circlet bears the text MISERERE · MEI · DEUS · SECUNDUM · MAGNAM · MISERICORDIAM · TUAM (Psalm 51.1). The use of this motto on heralds' crowns goes back to at least the reign of Queen Elizabeth I. One source says that since 1636 Garter has had a gold crown and the provincial Kings crowns of silver-gilt. However, although Anstis was Garter King of Arms this crown is silver-gilt. It is depicted in his portrait in the College of Arms.

Bibliography: Wagner, 1967, p. 91; Windsor, 1975, no. 108.
Lent by the Victoria and Albert Museum (Dept. of Metalwork no. M.4–1937).

102

101

103

IV
Civic, Corporate, Mercantile and Ecclesiastical Heraldry

Civic, Corporate and Mercantile

During the thirteenth century English cities and boroughs began to place shields of arms on their official seals. At first they consisted merely of the Royal arms, in reference to the King as overlord. In the latter years of the century they started to use their own distinctive heraldic devices, but it was not until the sixteenth century that municipal grants of arms were issued by the heralds.

Various factors determined the choice of charges. Quite often the emblem of a national saint, or a saint to whom the local cathedral or monastery was dedicated, or whose relics were housed there, was incorporated. In the case of the City of London both were taken into account as its arms are composed of the cross of St George and St Paul's sword (no. 124). Frequently the arms of the local seigneurial family were adopted; for example, the city of Chester has the same arms as the earldom of the same title (nos. 123, 224). Punning or canting arms occur, such as the ox crossing the ford, for the city of Oxford. Civic arms also make references to local trades and commercial interests; thus the Cinque Ports bore the pre-1340 Royal arms dimidiating three sailing ships.

In medieval towns and cities trade and craft guilds or companies existed, with religious and charitable functions as well as regulating conditions of work, wages and prices. The most important guilds, as one would expect, were in London. Their continental counterparts began to use armorial devices in the fourteenth century, but there is no evidence that this practice occurred in England before the second quarter of the fifteenth century. The earliest known grant of arms to a London company was that made to the Drapers in 1439 (no. 111), and between then and the end of the century no fewer than twenty-eight grants were issued by the heralds to London companies (no. 77). Many more were made in the sixteenth and seventeenth centuries, a period which also saw the granting of arms to the new trading companies established by royal charter to open up and exploit new markets overseas (nos. 113, 114). Most of these grants were given by Clarenceux King of Arms.

Many of the arms borne by the companies incorporate charges alluding to their individual crafts or trades, e.g. the buckles and cups of the Goldsmiths (no. 114) and the soldering-irons of the Plumbers (no. 119). Others make reference to the original religious dedications of the companies, such as the triple crowns resting on clouds of the Drapers, and the head of the Virgin on the Mercers' arms (nos. 111, 116). As a result of the doctrinal changes during the Reformation, some of the companies found it expedient to remove the religious devices; thus in the Brewers' grant made in 1544, the arms attributed to their patron saint, St Thomas of Canterbury, which had been included in the previous grant of 1468, were dropped from the new shield.

Individual members of a company frequently had its arms placed on their sepulchral monuments, particularly from the fifteenth into the seventeenth centuries (nos. 114, 116). With the development of an indigenous tin-glazed earthenware ceramic industry in the seventeenth century, arms of the companies appear on English pottery (nos. 112, 118); in the following century they are also found decorating porcelain services (no. 119).

Merchants also bore their own personal arms. At first, when armorial bearings were confined to the higher ranks of society, various devices known as merchants' marks were adopted by those engaged in commerce. There is a basic similarity between all the marks, but rarely are there two exactly alike. The earliest examples date from the end of the thirteenth century. They were primarily used to distinguish the goods of individual merchants, but also occur in a heraldic guise on monumental brasses (no. 104), rings (nos. 106, 107) and in the fabric and fittings of churches where they usually commemorate benefactors (no. 105). Although not recognised heraldic charges, merchants' marks were often placed on shields, sometimes in combination with company arms. This practice was disliked by the heralds. In 1530 Carlisle Herald visited various churches in the City of London '. . . to correct, deface and take away all manner of arms wrongfully borne or being false armory; or any marks or devices (such as Merchants' marks or Rebuses) put in escutcheons, squares or lozenges . . . against the laws of honour . . .' (Wagner, 1956, p. 119). The granting of arms to members of the mercantile classes became common in the sixteenth century, and the display of marks as pseudo-heraldry gradually declined during this and the following century. In the eighteenth century, the trade connections of certain merchants with the Far East led to the commissioning of services in Chinese porcelain decorated with armorial achievements copied from their bookplates (nos. 120, 121).

Ecclesiastical

From the fourteenth century, shields of arms were attributed to saints, dioceses and corporate ecclesiastical bodies, such as religious houses, hospitals and collegiate establishments. The assigning of heraldic charges to saints was in almost every case anachronistic, as the vast majority had been dead many centuries before the growth of heraldry. Frequently the arms devised included references to the saint's status (e.g. of royal blood, an abbot or abbess) and/or the symbols of suffering and martyrdom. Thus St Egwin (691–701) was given a shield of arms which included a chain and fetterlock and mitres, the latter signifying his office of Bishop of Worcester. In the very few cases when the saints were more recent, their family arms were adopted, e.g. St Thomas Cantilupe, Bishop of Hereford (1275–82), who was assigned the Cantilupe arms (Gules three leopards' heads inverted jessant de lis or). Mostly there does not seem to have been any *rationale* behind arms assigned to saints, such as the cross saltire of St Alban (no. 138) and the cross flory of St Edith (no. 127).

In certain dioceses, where the cathedral church was dedicated to a saint, his or her emblems were adopted as the arms of the See. Thus London has the crossed swords of St Paul's emblem of martyrdom (no. 128). Similarly, where there was an important local saint, the diocesan arms are frequently the same, as in the case of the See of Ely (no. 135), which has the same armorial bearings as those assigned to St Etheldreda. The new dioceses created after the Reformation (e.g. St Albans) often adopted arms attributed to their local saints. Apart from diocesan arms related to local or patron saints, ecclesiastical insignia such as mitres and pastoral staffs are frequently incorporated into the shields; just one example is the archbishop's pallium in the arms of the Province of Canterbury (no. 132). Sometimes religious iconography which had appeared on early episcopal seals would be incorporated into the arms of the diocese, e.g. the figure of Christ in Majesty for the See of Chichester. In other cases the choice of arms appears to have been as arbitrary as that for personal arms.

Similar principles governed the choice of heraldic charges for the pre-Reformation monasteries, friaries, colleges and hospitals which bore arms. Shields occur bearing the emblems of patron saints (no. 133) and, rather less commonly than in diocesan heraldry, some of the monastic houses included the ecclesiastical insignia of the pastoral staff in their arms (no. 128). There were several other considerations peculiar to corporate ecclesiastical heraldry. The arms of the lay founder of a monastery could appear on the official seal of that establishment (no. 137). There are also instances of a shield incorporating a device such as a gateway, referring to the geographical location of the house (no. 141). The subordinate priories or daughter-houses of large monasteries often used the arms of the mother-house (no. 138). Canting or punning arms appear to have been rare; one example is the rams' heads on the arms of Ramsey Abbey (no. 128). The shield of arms of Warden Abbey appears to be unique in that its charges refer to an item of produce (pears) for which the house was famed (no. 142).

Archbishops, bishops and the heads of religious houses could (and still may) impale their personal arms on the sinister side with those of their See or monastery (nos. 128, 129). Archbishops and bishops also ensign the shield with a mitre, and so too did the superiors of these monasteries which were granted the right to have pontificalian vestments. Finally, Cardinals of the pre-Reformation English Church bore their red hat of office over their personal arms (nos. 130, 131).

Much research remains to be done in the field of English ecclesiastical heraldry and the above remarks should be treated as only a very tentative introduction to the subject.

Select Bibliography

Bedford, W. K. R., *The Blazon of Episcopacy*, 2nd ed., Oxford, 1897.
Briggs, G., 'Diocesan Arms', *The Coat of Arms*, vi (1960–61), pp. 341–344; vii (1962–63), pp. 33–35, 75–78, 118–21, 149–52, 209–12, 334–36; viii (1964–65), pp. 37, 68–70.
Bromley, J., and Child, H., *The Armorial Bearings of the Guilds of London*, London, 1960.

Elmhirst, E. M., *Merchants' Marks*, The Harleian Society, cviii (1959).

Girling, F. A., *English Merchants' Marks*, London, 1962.

Hope, W. H. St John, 'English Municipal Heraldry', *Arch. J.*, lii (1895), pp. 173–97.

Hough, L. A., 'English Medieval Religious Heraldry', *The Coat of Arms*, xii (1970–71), pp. 76–80; New Series, i (1974), pp. 21–27.

Husenbeth, F. C., *Emblems of Saints*, 3rd ed., Norwich, 1882.

Pedrick, G., *Borough Seals of the Gothic Period*, London, 1904.

Plante, J., *Trades and Occupations shown on Rubbings of English Monumental Brasses from the 14th to the 18th century*, London, 1976.

Scott-Giles, C. W., *Civic Heraldry of England and Wales*, London, 1953.

104 Monumental Brass Shield with a Merchant's Mark, fifteenth century.
141 × 118 mm.

The shield has been used as a palimpsest, and on the obverse are the arms: Vair a chief checky. Found in the churchyard of Betchworth (Surrey).
Bibliography: Stephenson, 1903, p. 167; Stephenson, 1926, p. 577.
BM M&LA 1901, 3–9, 1. (Gift of Mill Stephenson)

105 Relief Tile with a Merchant's Mark, fifteenth or sixteenth century.
W 110 mm.

The merchant's mark, which is set on a shield, has been incorrectly interpreted as the arms of the Passion. The design occurs several times in the pavement from Burton Lazars displayed in the Medieval Tile and Pottery Room.
Found on the site of the leper hospital of Burton Lazars (Leics.).
Bibliography: Whitcomb, 1956, no. 249.
BM M&LA tile no. 4746.

106 Finger-ring with a Merchant's Mark, fifteenth–sixteenth century.
Gold; D of hoop 27 mm.

The hoop is engraved with the name HENRY SMALE in 'black-letter'.
Bibliography: Dalton, 1912, no. 356, Pl. VI.
BM M&LA Franks Bequest No. 657.

107 Finger-ring with a Merchant's Mark, early sixteenth century.
Gold; D of hoop 28 mm.

The shoulders of the ring bear the name IOHANS FRESCI in 'black-letter'.
Found in the Thames at Southwark Bridge.
Bibliography: Dalton, 1912, no. 355, Pl. VI.
BM M&LA Franks Bequest No. 656.

108 Seal Matrix of the Mayor of the Staple of Westminster, 1393.
Silver; D 53 mm.

The central device is two keys in saltire between four wool packs. The legend reads SIGILLU: OFFICII:

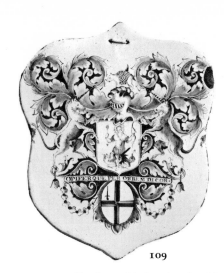

109

MAIORATUS: WESTMONASTERII. Staples were towns through which, for fiscal reasons, wool, hides and lead were exported. The Staple at Westminster was established in 1353. An impression of the seal of the Mayor is known dated 1366 and this, though smaller, bears the same device. This silver matrix was probably made in 1393 when the ordinance creating the Staples was confirmed. The devices of seals of mayors of the Staples in the fourteenth century usually combine royal elements such as the leopard or fleur-de-lis with local references such as the crossed keys for Westminster. Wool packs occur on the seals for Boston and Lincoln as well as Westminster.
Bibliography: W. de G. Birch, 'Communication to the Society of Antiquaries', *Proc. Soc. Ants.*, xii (1887–89), pp. 245–46; H. S. Kingsford, 'Seal matrices in the University Museum of Archaeology and Ethnology, Cambridge', *Proc. Cambridge Antiq. Soc.*, xxx (1927–8), pp. 16–28; Tonnochy, 1952, no. 36.
BM M&LA 88, 11–18, 1. (Gift of A. W. Franks)

109 Pill Tile with the Arms of the Worshipful Society of Apothecaries of London, early eighteenth century. Tin-glazed earthenware ('delftware'), in the form of a shield; 308 × 257 mm.

Painted in blue with the arms of the Society (Apollo proper with his head radiant holding in his left hand a bow and in his right hand an arrow, supplanting a serpent), crest, mantling, supporters and motto: OPIFERQUE PER ORBEM DICOR; below, an oval shield with the arms of the City of London. Made with two pierced and glazed holes for hanging, probably in an apothecary's shop to indicate that the owner was a freeman of his Society. Probably made in Lambeth. The Society was incorporated and the arms granted by William Camden, Clarenceux, in 1617.
Bibliography: Hobson, 1903, no. E70, Pl. XI; Tilley, 1967, pp. 265–66; L. G. Matthews, 'Apothecaries' Pill Tiles', *Trans. English Ceramic Circle*, 7, pt. 3 (1970), pp. 200–209.
BM M&LA Franks Coll., 1887.

110 Medallion with the Arms of the Cooks' Company, eighteenth century.
Silver-gilt; D 44 mm.

The obverse is engraved with the arms of the Company (a chevron engrailed between three columbine flowers), supported by a buck and doe, each transfixed by an arrow. On the reverse is inscribed: ROBERT BAXTER, ADMITTED ON THE LIVERY, 4 JULY 1799. The arms were granted by William Hawkeslowe, Clarenceux King of Arms, in 1467.
Bibliography: *Montague Guest Cat.*, no. 917, Pl. IV.
BM M&LA Montague Guest No. 917.

110

111 Grant of Arms to the Worshipful Company of Drapers, 1439. Vellum; 460 × 522 mm.

Grant in French by Sir William Bruges, Garter King of Arms. The grant is framed by decorated borders and in the initial is depicted the Virgin of Mercy crowned as Queen of Heaven; at the top is a shield with the Company's arms (Azure three sunbeams issuing from clouds gules crowned with three imperial crowns or), supported by two kneeling angels; Bruges' seal in red wax is appended. This charter, which is not only the earliest grant to a City company, but the oldest known surviving English patent of arms, was granted by Bruges on 10 March, 1439. There is a close relationship in the style of the illumination with no. 212, and the two works have been attributed to the same artist.
Bibliography: HCEC., no. 62; Wagner, 1946, p. 30, Pl. VIII; Wagner, 1956, p. 75; S. Goodall, 'Heraldry and Iconography. A study of the arms granted to the Drapers' Company of London', *The Coat of Arms*, iv (1956–57), pp. 170–83; Bromley and Child, 1960, pp. 73–77, Pl. 18; T. Girtin, *The Triple Crowns*, London, 1964, pp. 54–56 and col. frontispiece; Alexander, 1972, p. 169.
Lent by the Worshipful Company of Drapers.

111

**112 Puzzle Cup or Table-fountain
with the Arms of the Worshipful
Company of Drapers,** 1674.
Tin-glazed earthenware ('delftware'),
with a detachable syphon (incomplete) in centre of bowl; H 247
mm.

Painted in blue with the arms of the
Company and the initials and date:
I.W. 1674. Made in London, at
Southwark or Lambeth, it is the
only known example of this type of
vessel extant. These arms were first
granted in 1439 (see no. 111).
Bibliography: Hodgkin, 1891, no.
341; Hobson, 1903, no. E 13, Pl.
XII; Tilley, 1967, p. 126, fig. 3;
Amsterdam, 1973, no. 46.
BM M&LA Franks Coll., 1887.

**113 Seal Matrix of the Eastland
Company,** 1579.
Silver, D 68·5 mm (hinged and
pierced semi-circular handle on
reverse).

The matrix is engraved with the
Company arms (on the sea in base
a ship of three masts with sails,
pennants and ensigns charged with
a cross, and on a chief a lion
passant guardant). The shield is
supported by two bears and the
crest is an ass-camel; below is a
scroll bearing the motto DISPAIR
NOT. At the top is the date 1579. In
that year the Company was founded
by Royal charter to oppose the
Hanseatic Steelyard merchants'
monopoly of the Baltic trade.
Bibliography: Tonnochy, 1952, no.
155.
BM M&LA 1928, 3–15, 2.

**114 Monumental Brass Shield with
the Arms of the Goldsmiths'
Company,** sixteenth century.
124 × 104 mm.

The arms (Quarterly, 1 and 4, a
leopard's head, 2 and 3, a covered
cup and two buckles) have been
used by the Company since the late
fifteenth century. This shield is one
of the earliest bearing these arms
to be found on a brass.
From a memorial to the Latham
family at Upminster (Essex).
Bibliography: BHA., p. 8, Pl. IV;

I

116

Stephenson, 1926, pp. 139, 577.
BM M&LA 1920, 4–15, 3.

115 Plate with the Arms of the Worshipful Company of Joiners, 1776.

Tin-glazed earthenware ('delftware'), in octagonal form; 217 × 216 mm.

Painted in blue with the arms of the Company (a chevron between in chief two compasses extended and in base a globe, on a chief a pale between two roses, on the pale an escallop), crest, mantling, supporters and motto: Joyn Loyalty & Liberty. On the reverse, the date (in blue): 1776. These arms were granted by Robert Cooke, Clarenceux, in 1571.
Bibliography: Tilley, 1968, p. 129, Fig. 12.
BM M&LA 1932, 3–14, I. (Gift of Mr John E. Pritchard)

116 Monumental Brass Shield with the Arms of the Mercers' Company, sixteenth century.

148 × 119 mm.

The shield bears the Virgin couped at the neck within a bordure of clouds. The facial features are indicated by painted lines, but possibly originally the face was enamelled. The arms are derived from the Virgin device used on a Company seal of 1393.
Bibliography: Stephenson, 1926, p. 577.
BM M&LA 75, 1–20, 6.

117 Seal Matrix of the Muscovy Merchants, 1555.

Silver; D 51 mm (hinged semi-circular handle on the reverse).

The matrix bears the Company's arms (Barry wavy of six, overall a ship of three masts, with sails, pennants and ensigns charged with a cross, all between three roundels, and in chief on a pale between two roses a lion passant guardant). Over the shield is the date 1555 and the rim inscription reads: +REFVGIVM NOSTRVM IN DEO. In 1555 a Royal charter was granted to a joint-stock company to trade with Russia, a sea-route to which had been opened up by Chancellor's voyage of 1553. The first governor of the Merchants was Sebastian Cabot.
Bibliography: Tonnochy, 1952, no. 158.
BM M&LA 1928, 3–15, I.

117

118 Dish with the Arms of the Worshipful Company of Pewterers, 1655.
Tin-glazed earthenware ('delftware'), with moulded decoration in imitation of the 'cut-card' ornamentation on contemporary silver dishes; D 421 mm.

Painted in blue and yellow with the arms of the Company (on a chevron between three strikes, as many roses), a set of three initials and the date: ₁S₁ 1655. Probably made in Southwark to commemorate a marriage, the surname of the bridegroom commencing with 's'. The arms were granted by Thomas Benolt, Clarenceux, in 1533.
Bibliography: Hodgkin, 1891, no. 287; Hobson, 1903, no. E 51, Pl. XII; Tilley, 1967, p. 268, Fig. 5.
BM M&LA Franks Coll., 1888.

119 Spoon-tray with the Arms of the Worshipful Company of Plumbers, *c.* 1770.
Porcelain, painted in colours, with gilding; 154 × 88 mm.

Painted with the arms of the Company (Or on a chevron sable between in chief a slide-rule between two sounding leads argent and in base a water-level; on the chevron two soldering-irons in saltire between a cutting-knife and a shaver argent), crest and the mottoes: JUSTITIA ET PAX and IN GOD IS ALL OUR HOPE. Part of a service (now dispersed) made at Worcester about 1770 but possibly decorated in London at the workshop of James Giles. No reference to this service has yet been found in the records of the Company. The arms were granted by Robert Cooke, Clarenceux, in 1588.
Bibliography: Marshall, 1946, pp. 199–200.
BM M&LA 1942, 4–11, 5. (The Revd G. A. Schneider Bequest)

119

120 Milk Jug with the Arms of Barnwell, *c.* 1745.
Porcelain, decorated in enamels;
H 120 mm.

The jug bears the arms of Barnwell (Gules a saltire embattled between four crescents argent) with crest and motto LOYAL AU MOAT (correctly MORT). Part of a service made in China during the reign of the Ch'ien-lung emperor (1736–95), Ch'ing dynasty, for Michael Barnwell (d. 1792) of the East India Company. The arms are taken from the family's bookplate (no. 121).
Bibliography: Howard, 1974, p. 416.
BM OA Franks 780+.

121 Engraved Armorial Bookplate of the Barnwell Family, eighteenth century.
120 × 92 mm.

This bookplate provided the source for the shield of arms on no. 120.
Bibliography: Book Plates Cat., i, no. 1580.
BM P&D Bookplates no 1580.

121

120

122 Plate with the Arms of Salter impaling Brooke, *c.* 1730. Porcelain, decorated in underglaze blue and enamels; D 384 mm.

The arms (Gules ten billets argent, 4, 3, 2 and 1, within a bordure engrailed of the second impaling Or a cross engrailed per pale gules and sable), mantling and crest are those of Sir John Salter (d. 1744). He was Lord Mayor of London in 1740 and was a director of the East India Company. The plate was made in China during the reign of the Yung-cheng emperor (1723–35), Ch'ing dynasty.

Bibliography: Tudor-Craig, 1925, p. 87; Howard, 1974, p. 173; Kodansha, *Oriental Ceramics, The World's Great Collections* Vol. 5. *The British Museum*, Tokyo, 1975, pl. 71.

BM OA 1887, 12–18, 33 (Franks 735+). (Revd C. H. Walker Bequest)

123 Punch Bowl with the Badge of the Prince of Wales, the Arms of the Duchy of Cornwall, the Cities of Chester and Plymouth, and the Baron of Renfrew.

Porcelain, painted in colours, with gilding and inscribed:

SPODE AND COPELAND
Manufacturer's (*sic*)
Feb[y]. 1813.
D 412 mm; H 174 mm.

This highly emblematical bowl, with its diverse painted inscriptions totalling 1,168 words, is self-styled 'A REGENCY BOWL.' and is a veritable *tour de force*. Presented in November 1813 by Mr William Rogers, in the name of the Cornwall Topographical and Caledonian Society, to the British Museum, it bears the names of the forty Trustees, the ten qualified members of the staff and the names of the four Departments then in existence. It is an eloquent plea to persons of exalted rank and influence to obtain 'liberal patronage' for the economically depressed china-clay industry of the St Stephen-in-Brannel district of Cornwall, hit by Napoleon's and the United States's embargo on all British goods (since 1806). Mr William Rogers, of Treneague, near St Austell, seems not only to have founded this curious Society in 1808 to help achieve this aim but also to have planned to establish in Cornwall a manufactory of porcelain; to this day, there remains a conviction among many Cornishmen that, if not this 'Regency Bowl', at least some of the other less spectacular pieces produced for Rogers' campaign were actually made in St Austell. By 1813 Messrs Spode and Copeland was among the leading firms in the Potteries and since 1799 had been the principal leasee of Carloggas Moor, near St Stephen-in-Brannel, working the pits and exporting vast quantities of clay and stone to the factory in Stoke for the production of its new bone-china wares.
Bibliography: Hobson, 1905, no. XIV.8; H. Tait, 'Spode and Copeland: "A Regency Bowl" dated 1813', *The Connoisseur*, clxxiv (1970), pp. 24–33.
BM M&LA Donations Book, 1813.

124

124 Snuff-box Presented by the City of London to Sir Robert Peel, 1829.
Gold, with London hall-mark for 1828–29; L 100 mm, W 70 mm, H 27 mm.

The lid bears the arms of the City of London (a cross and on the dexter chief a sword erect), with crest, supporters and motto. On the base are the arms of Sir Robert Peel (three sheaves of as many arrows banded, on a chief a bee volant) with crest and the motto INDUSTRIA. The lid and sides are embellished with foliage in relief. Inside the lid is an engraved inscription recording that the box and the Freedom of the City were conferred on Peel for his efforts to secure emancipation for Roman Catholics. Sir Robert Peel (1788–1850) was at the time Home Secretary in the Tory administration; ironically he had for long been opposed to granting emancipation to Catholics.
BM M&LA 1921, 6–18, I. (Gift of Lady Emily Peel)

125 Seal Matrix of the Vicar of the Franciscan Custos, Cambridge, early fourteenth century.
Bronze; H 45 mm (pointed oval, ridge and loop handle on reverse).

The matrix is engraved with a shield bearing the arms of Christ's Passion (a cross raguly pierced by three nails, debruised by a spear and crown of thorns in bend, and a sponge on a spear in bend sinister with two scourges in base). Above is a crocketed double canopy and below the Vicar kneeling in prayer within a cusped niche. Legend (in Lombardic script): s'. VICARII CVSTODIS CANTEBRIGGIE. This appears to be the earliest English representation of the 'Arma Christi'.
Bibliography: Tonnochy, 1952, no. 836; A. G. Little (ed.), *Franciscan History and Legend in English Mediaeval Art*, Manchester, 1937, p. 85.
BM M&LA 58, 2–18, 2.

126 Inlaid Tile showing the 'Arma Christi', mid-fifteenth century.
H 218 mm.

From the Priory church at Great Malvern (Worcs.). The version of the arms of Christ on this tile consists of the cross with nails above and scourges beneath between a spear dexter and a ladder sinister. The tile is one of a set of five rectangular wall tiles of which a complete set can be seen in the Medieval Tile and Pottery Room. This includes a canopy above which is the date 36 Henry VI (1457–58). The other tiles have the sacred monogram IHS crowned, the Royal arms, and the Pelican in her Piety.
Bibliography: Nichols, 1845, no. 68; Eames, 1968, Colour Plate C.
BM M&LA tile no. 1330.

127 Instructions for Glazing the Observant Friars' Church, Greenwich, *c.* 1490–94.
Vellum; 1·75 × 0·155 m.

One of two rolls providing detailed instructions to a glass-painter for a series of figures with shields of arms above and below the transom. The large number of figures suggests that the window was probably at either the east or the west end of the Observants' church. The figures include kings and saints such as Louis King of France, Ethelbert and Edith, and the arms attributed to them are painted in the left margin. The Greenwich house of the Observants, or reformed Franciscans, was founded by Edward IV, but the church was not built until Henry VII's reign; it appears to have been completed in 1493–4. It is now only known from Wyngaerde's drawings of 1558.
Bibliography: Hasted's History of

Kent, Pt. i The Hundred of Blackheath, ed. H. H. Drake, London, 1886, pp. 86–87, n. 6; A. R. Martin, *Franciscan Architecture in England,* Manchester, 1937, p. 238.
BL Egerton MS. 2341A.

128 Peers Spiritual in the Parliament Procession Roll of 1512, early seventeenth century copy.
Vellum; 0·3 × 5·6 m.

A painted roll showing King Henry VIII walking in procession to the Parliament of 1512. The King, attended by the officers of state, is preceded by the spiritual peers and officers of arms, and followed by the lords temporal. The figures, processing in pairs, are identified by their arms and by their names on scrolls above their heads. The ecclesiastical arms show personal arms impaling arms of the diocese or religious house. The roll is the forerunner of the Parliament rolls

(see e.g. no. 129) compiled by Garter King of Arms to record the names and arms in order of precedence of lords who took their seats on the first day of a Parliament.
This copy of the Parliament Procession Roll is artistically inferior to a sixteenth century version (possibly prepared for Sir Thomas Wriothesley, Garter) in Trinity College, Cambridge (MS.0.3.59), but has fewer of the identifying shields left blank. A further seventeenth century copy is Bodleian Library Ashmolean MS. 12., and an eighteenth century copy of the present roll, by the Revd William Cole, the Cambridgeshire antiquary, is in BL Additional MS. 5831.
Bibliography: Eden, 1934, pp. 363–66; HCEC., no. 15; Wagner and Sainty, 1967, pp. 128, 142–50, Pls. XVII–XX; Wagner, 1967, p. 149, Pl. XIV.
BL Additional MS. 22306.

128

129 Arms of Peers Spiritual in the Parliament Roll, 1515.
Vellum; 4·6 × 0·209 m.

A roll of arms of the Sovereign and lords spiritual and temporal who sat in the Parliament held at Westminster, 5 February 1514/1515. Made for Sir Thomas Wriothesley, Garter, as one of a series of Parliament rolls (see no. 128). Beneath the Royal arms the shields are painted in two columns with names over, those of the spiritual peers showing their personal and official arms impaled beneath a mitre.

A copy made in 1640 when the roll belonged to Sir William le Neve, Clarenceux, is among the Hatton-Dugdale facsimiles (see no. 58). In 1829 Thomas Willement, the heraldic artist and antiquary, published the roll in facsimile while it was in his possession.
Bibliography: Eden, 1934, p. 366; HCEC., nos. 13–15, Pl. XXX; Wagner and Sainty, 1967, p. 128. BL Additional MS. 40078.

130 Snuffers of Cardinal Bainbridge, Archbishop of York, 1511–14.
Silver, parcel-gilt and enamelled; 160 × 56 × 24 mm.

The snuffers bear the Royal arms of England surmounted by a crown and the arms of Bainbridge (Quarterly, 1 and 4, Azure two battle-axes in pale or and on a chief or two mullets gules pierced of the field; 2 and 3, Gules a squirrel or) surmounted by a Cardinal's hat and archiepiscopal staff. The sides of the snuffers and the junction and terminals to the handles have devices taken from the Bainbridge arms. Bainbridge was Henry VIII's resident ambassador to the Papal Curia in Rome. The characteristically Tudor form of the crown over the Royal arms and the lack of any Renaissance motifs point to an English, rather than an Italian, origin for the snuffers. If so, they are the earliest surviving English snuffers.
Bibliography: C. J. Jackson, *An Illustrated History of English Plate*, ii, London, 1911, p. 877; C. Oman,

129

'A Pair of Tudor Snuffers', *Burl. Mag.*, liii (1928), p. 295; A. J. Collins (ed.), *Jewels and Plate of Queen Elizabeth I*, London, 1955, p. 39.
BM M&LA 78, 12–30, 633. (Henderson Bequest)

Colour plate

131 Painted Arms of Cardinal Wolsey, 1515–30.
Paper; 245 × 189 mm.

Painting of the arms of Cardinal Wolsey (d. 1530), against a blue background framed by Renaissance motifs. On a shield are the arms: Sable on a cross engrailed argent four leopards' heads azure and a lion passant gules and on a chief or a rose gules between two Cornish choughs sable. The shield is surmounted by a Cardinal's hat and supported by two griffins holding small pillars; behind are two archiepiscopal crosses in saltire and above the arms is the Holy Spirit. Said to be the earliest known English book-plate, but there is no certainty that it has always been associated with the book in which it is pasted (*Tomus Primus Quatuor Conciliorum generalium*, ed. Jacques Merlin, Paris, 1524).
Bibliography: W. J. Hardy, *Book-Plates*, London, 1897, pp. 18, 24, 26; Croft-Murray and Hulton, 1960, p. xxviii.
BL C. 37. l. 8.

132 Seal Matrix of the Vicar-General of the Archbishop of Canterbury, early seventeenth century.
Silver; H 96 mm (pointed oval).

The matrix is engraved with the arms of the Archbishop (a cross-staff in pale, surmounted by a pallium charged with four crosses formy fitchy) surmounted by a mitre.
Legend: THE · SEAL · OF · THE · VICAR · GENERAL · TO · HIS · GRACE · OF · CANTERBURY ·
BM M&LA 1963, 4–3, 3. (Gift of Mrs E. W. Fuller in memory of her husband)

133 Seal Matrix of John Sante, Abbot of Abingdon and Papal Commissary, 1469–95.
Bronze; H 91 mm (pointed oval, pierced handle).

The matrix depicts the Virgin and Child flanked by ss. Peter and Paul under tall canopies. Below are three shields of arms: a lion rampant (the arms of Sante?), an oak tree eradicated (the arms of Pope Sixtus IV, a member of the della Rovere family, whose diplomatic representative the Abbot was), and a cross patonce between four Cornish choughs (Abingdon Abbey). The last coat was borrowed from that assigned to the local saint, Edmund of Abingdon. Legend (in 'black-letter'): SIGILLV̄ : DN̄I : IOH̄IS : ABBATIS : ABENDONIE : S : D : N : PAPE : COMMISSARII.
Bibliography: Tonnochy, 1952, no. 828; J. Goodall, 'The Seal-Die of John Sante, Abbot of Abingdon', *The Coat of Arms*, iv (1956–57), pp. 105–106.
BM M&LA 50, 9–24, 7. (Gift of Lady Fellows)

134 Double Seal Matrix of the Bishopric of Durham during Vacancy of the See, 1437–38.
Bronze; D 76 mm (circular, each half with four loops).

The obverse is engraved with the equestrian figure of Henry VI with his surcoat, shield and the caparisons of the horse charged with the Royal arms of England (Quarterly France modern and England). On the field is a shield of arms with the arms of St Oswald/ the See of Durham (a cross between four lions rampant). The ground below the horse shows the 'planta genista', for the Plantagenet rulers of England. Legend, in 'black-letter': S. HENRICI DEI GRA REG ANGL' & FRANC' & DN̄I HIBN̄ PRO EPTŪ · DUNOLM̄ · SEDE · VOCANTE. The reverse bears a shield with the Royal arms; the legend repeats that on the obverse.
During the vacancy of a diocese, i.e. when there was no bishop, its temporalities were held by the King. The Bishopric of Durham was an independent palatinate over which

131 ▷

the King normally had no jurisdiction. This presumably explains
the need for a special seal to be
engraved bearing the Royal arms
for the administration of the See
during the vacancy.
Bibliography: Tonnochy, 1952, no.
824.
BM MLA 1842, No. 1. (Gift of the
Lords of the Treasury)

**135 Shield with the Arms of the
Diocese of Ely,** early sixteenth
century.
Stained glass; 368 × 318 mm.

The shield bears Gules three crowns
or and has blue, green, red and
purple mantling above and below.
These arms are also attributed to
St Etheldreda (d. 679), whose
shrine was in Ely Cathedral.
From Barham Hall (Suffolk).
Bibliography: Rackham, 1936, p. 60.
Lent by the Victoria and Albert
Museum (Dept of Ceramics no.
C.796–1920).

**136 Tile with the Arms of
Gloucester Abbey,** fourteenth–
fifteenth century.
W 127 mm.

This tile bears the arms of
Gloucester Abbey (two keys in
saltire wards upwards, overall a
sword in pale hilt upwards).
Gloucester Abbey was dedicated to
ss. Peter and Paul and this explains
the choice of the keys (St Peter) and
sword (St Paul).
From Blithfield church (Staffs.).
BM M&LA tile no. 1509.

**137 Double Seal Matrix of
Haltemprice Priory (Yorks.),** 1322.
Bronze; D 76 mm (circular, each
half with four loops).

The obverse is engraved with a
representation of a church and the
arms of Wake (two bars and in
chief three roundels) repeated three
times, of Stuteville (Barry of twelve)
and a shield bearing a cross patonce.
On the reverse is depicted a three-
storeyed architectural structure
containing the Crucifixion, censing
angels, ss. Peter and Paul, the Prior
and five canons; the structure is
flanked by the kneeling figures of

the founder, Thomas, Lord Wake,
and his wife. On his ailettes, two
standards and a shield are the
Wake arms. The French inscription
on the reverse has the date 1322.
This matrix provides an
example of a religious house whose
arms were borrowed from those of
the founder. Thomas Wake, Lord of
Liddell, established the Priory in
1322. The arms of the Stutevilles
are included since their heiress was
a great-grandmother of the founder.
Bibliography: Tonnochy, 1952, no.
841.
BM M&LA 1913, 11–5, 2.

**138 Seal Matrix of Hatfield
Peverel Priory (Essex),** fourteenth
century.
Bronze; H 68 mm (pointed oval,
projecting pierced handle on
reverse).

The matrix depicts the Virgin and
Child seated within a canopied
niche and flanked by two shields of
arms, one bearing three annulets,
the other a saltire. 'Black-letter'
legend: SIGILLŪ CŌE ECCLESIE BEATE
MARIE DE HATFELD PEVELL. The
second shield bears the same arms
as St Alban/St Albans Abbey, of
which Hatfield Peverel was a
dependent priory.
Bibliography: BHA., p. 110;
Tonnochy, 1952, no. 842.
BM M&LA 1920, 4–15, 11.

**139 Tile with the Arms of the See
of Lichfield,** fifteenth century.
W 118 mm.

This tile shows a cross potent
quadrant between four crosses formy,
which are the arms of Lichfield
diocese. The cross potent is first
associated with the See of Lichfield
on the seal of Bishop William Booth
(1447–52).
From Maxstoke Priory (Warwicks.).
Bibliography: Whitcomb, 1956, no.
168.
BM M&LA tile no. 2568.

**140 Seal Matrix for Ecclesiastical
Jurisdiction in the Archdeaconry of
Norfolk,** 1547–53.
Bronze; H 87 mm (pointed oval).

The matrix is engraved with the
Royal arms as used by the Tudors,
supported by a lion and a wyvern.
On a label below is PRO · ARCHINATV
NORFF. Legend: +SIGILLVM: REGIE:
MAIESTATIS: AD: CAVSAS:
ECCLESIASTICAS. This matrix is one
of several still surviving made in
conformity with a 1547 statute,
which laid down that ecclesiastical
jurisdiction was to be exercised in
the name of the Crown. It stated
that all those exercising this
jurisdiction '. . . shall have . . . in
their seales of office the kinges
highnesse armes decently set, with
certeine caracts under the armes
for the knowledge of the diocese'.
The statute was repealed by Queen
Mary I in 1553.
Bibliography: Tonnochy, 1952, no.
809.
BM M&LA 68, 3–18, 12. (Gift of
A. W. Franks)

**141 Seal Matrix of St Leonard's
Leper Hospital, Northampton,**
fifteenth century.
Bronze; 64 mm (pointed oval,
projecting pierced handle on
reverse).

The matrix depicts St Leonard
standing within a canopied niche.
On the shield of arms below is a
barbican gateway with a crown in
chief. The 'black-letter' legend
reads: S · COE · DOMUS · SCI ·
LEONARDI · IUXTA · NORHAMPTON.
The gateway probably represents
the location of the Hospital near
the south gate of the town and the
crown symbolizes its royal foundation.
Bibliography: Tonnochy, 1952, no.
848.
BM M&LA 1936, 10–15, 4.

**142 Circular Plaque with the Arms
of Warden Abbey (Beds.),** fifteenth
century.
Copper-gilt and enamelled; D 118
mm.

The plaque shows the Virgin and
Child seated in a niche under a
crocketed triple canopy and flanked
by two shields bearing the Abbey's
arms (Azure three pears or) on a
red ground. The rim consists of

conjoined angels emerging from clouds. This plaque, which may have been a morse, is one of three found near Shefford (Beds.). The Cistercian Abbey of Warden was famed for its pears, which thus provided the charges for the arms. *Bibliography:* M. Chamot, *English Mediaeval Enamels*, London, 1930, no. 21.
BM M&LA 53, 6–7, 1.

142

V
Personal Arms

As was stated in the Introduction to Early Heraldry, the display of shields of arms in all branches of artistic activity reached its apogee during the reigns of Henry VII and Henry VIII. The almost total cessation of church building caused by the Reformation drastically reduced the opportunities for architectural heraldry within an ecclesiastical context. In the Elizabethan and Jacobean age, however, arms continued to be represented in church windows and on tombs. In fact, this period saw a more lavish and ostentatious application of heraldic achievements on funerary monuments than ever before. Throughout the fifteenth and early sixteenth centuries, shields of arms had tended to become more and more elaborate in their quarterings; during the second half of the sixteenth and early seventeenth centuries this trend rapidly accelerated and frequently resulted in tombs with numerous overcrowded shields, designed to show the remotest family alliances and ancestries of the deceased. This desire to parade family connections also led to the production of elaborately decorated pedigrees, such as that of the Hesketh family (no. 148). There was less room on small personal belongings such as seals and rings for shields with many quarterings, and most of those of this period are simple (nos. 149–151, 153); nevertheless, the seal of Richard Towneley shows that sometimes very complex shields do occur (no. 152).

After the Civil War and Commonwealth, which saw much destruction and defacement of tombs, lavish heraldic embellishment of monuments went out of fashion. This loss, however, was largely made good by the displaying of large funeral hatchments in churches, a practice which had first come into vogue in the early seventeenth century. Moreover, from the sixteenth century the increasing accumulation of personal possessions by the well-to-do opened up new fields for armorial decoration. Ceramics and plate were particularly suited for such treatment. With regard to the former, in the seventeenth century, shields of arms were largely confined to tin-glazed earthenware, commonly known as 'delftware' (nos. 155–157). Armorial pottery continued to be manufactured in the following century, but it was largely superseded in popularity by porcelain services. As was illustrated in the preceding section, much porcelain was commissioned from China, with bookplates (themselves a common medium for heraldic display from the sixteenth century) being sent out to provide the correct armorial designs (nos. 159–162). Numerous services bearing shields of arms were also ordered from the English porcelain factories; some of the finest examples were produced at Worcester (nos. 163–165, 170).

The tomb of Sir John Spencer (d. 1586) in Great Brington church (Northants.), made by Jasper Hollemans (see cat. no. 83)

Silver has from very early times been a popular medium for the display of arms. This is particularly true of commemorative or presentation plate, such as the cups Sir Nicholas Bacon had made from the Great Seal of Philip and Mary (no. 146). In addition, those who could afford table silver often had their arms engraved or embossed on it. Much of the British Museum's fine collection of eighteenth century silver made by refugee Huguenot gold-smiths for English patrons bears heraldic achievements; one of the most spectacular examples is the dish made by Paul de Lamerie for George Treby (no. 158).

Whatever the medium in which shields of arms were displayed in this period, usually they were enclosed by mantling or some sort of framing. The style of the latter was determined by the prevailing ornamental fashion of the day. In the late Elizabethan and Jacobean eras strapwork was an almost universal framing device (nos. 146, 154), whereas for much of the eighteenth century elaborate Rococo cartouches were adopted (no. 158). In the same century the shield often ceased to be recognizable as an item of martial equipment and became merged with its surround (nos. 161–163, 165). Towards the end of the eighteenth century the Gothic Revival movement resulted in the re-emergence of the heater-shaped shield of medieval times (nos. 170, 232).

As for purely heraldic development, the early Tudor period was an age of crowded shields, with chevrons and chiefs commonly bearing charges; this is shown particularly well by the Parliament Procession Roll of 1512 and the seals of the Eastland and Muscovy companies, displayed in the previous section (nos. 128, 113, 117). Under Queen Elizabeth, in contrast with the elaborate heraldic quarterings and impalings on contemporary funerary monuments, newly granted arms demonstrate a return to simpler and fewer charges, such as those of Sir Nicholas Bacon (no. 144). This trend lasted until the middle of the eighteenth century, when the fashion began of introducing pictorial compositions as heraldic charges; the results can be judged from the cup and saucer bearing the arms of Lord Nelson (no. 171). As Sir Anthony Wagner has justly remarked, these pictorial com-positions are 'wholly foreign to the genius of heraldry'.

The Colour Plates

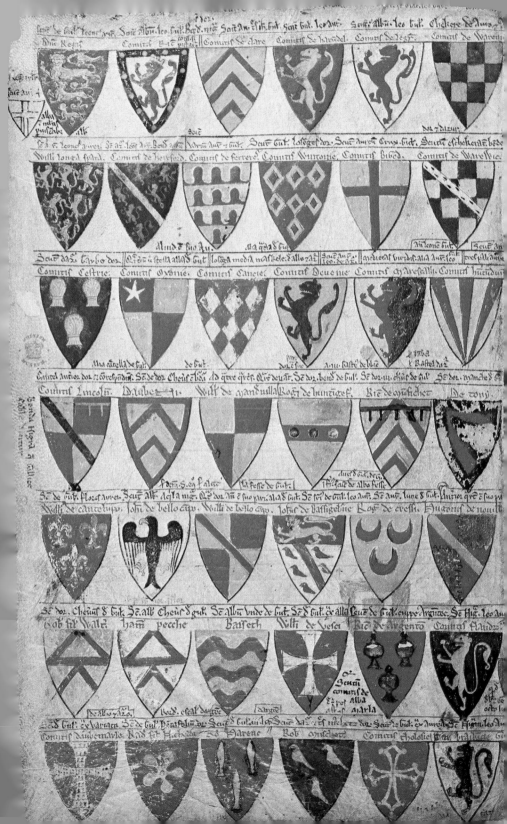

14 △　△88　　　　　　　　　　　　　▽70

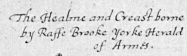

The Healme and Creast borne
by Raffe Brooke Yorke Herald
of Armes.

Robert Treswell Somersett &
John Rauen Richmond Heralds
of Armes.

The great
Earle of

Embrotherud Barnty of England bornt by ye
Pembroke assisted by the Lo: Howard of Effingh—

The Targett borne by
[...] Thomas Chester
[He]rald of Armes.

The Sword borne by
William Segar Norroy
King of Armes.

A Gentleman
Usher with a
white Rodd

The Coate borne by
William Cambden
Clarenceux King
of Armes.

A Gentleman
Usher with a
white rodd.

Paintings of the
Ceremony of Knight-
hood of the Bath,
c. 1488

144

143 Confirmation of Arms to Robert Stywarde, 1558.
Vellum; 610 × 840 mm.

This certificate, in Latin, by William Harvey, Clarenceux King of Arms 1557–67, for Robert Stywarde of Ely (d. 1570), attests the descent of the Stywarde *al.* Steward family from the Scottish Royal House of Stewart, and their right to bear the Stewart arms (Or a fess checky argent and azure), instead of an existing family coat of Stywarde (Argent a lion gules debruised by a ragged staff or). This claim of an obscure family of Norfolk origins to an imposing royal genealogy (itself largely fictitious), and to the Stewart arms, was exposed as fraudulent in the nineteenth century by, among others, the formidable historian and genealogist J. H. Round.

The Stywarde family concocted an elaborate story to explain the awkward fact that the arms they bore were wholly different from the Stewart coat. The account involved the exploits of a Stewart ancestor who slew the lion of Balliol with a ragged staff, and in return received from Charles VI of France the right to bear the lion and staff as an augmentation of honour on the Stewart arms. This incident is depicted in the top margin. A grant by an earlier herald gave them the right to use the lion coat either as an augmentation or alone. In the present charter Clarenceux has been induced to accept the explanation for the disappearance of the Stewart arms in the Stywarde 'branch' of the family, and confirms their right to resume the coat of arms of their alleged ancestors.

His picture in the initial holding the two shields bears the appropriate motto '*Utrum mavis elige*' (Choose which you prefer).
Bibliography: J. H. Round, *Studies in Peerage and Family History*, London, 1901, pp. 131–46.
BL Additional MS. 59865.

144 Exemplification of Arms and Grant of Crest to Sir Nicholas Bacon, 1569.
Vellum; 365 × 650 mm.

The arms here confirmed to Sir Nicholas Bacon (d. 1579), Lord Keeper, by Sir Gilbert Dethick, Garter, Robert Cooke, Clarenceux, and William Flower, Norroy, are painted in the left-hand margin: Quarterly 1 and 4 for Bacon, Gules on a chief argent two mullets sable; 2 and 3 for Quaplade, Barry of six or and azure, overall a bend gules. The crest is described 'on a Torce silver and gueules a Bore passant ermyne: Mantelyd asure, doublid golde: as more playnely appeerith depicted in his margent'. Decoration in the other margins includes impaled or quartered coats of several generations of the family (Ufford, Quaplade, Ferneley, Cooke). The initial letter encloses a portrait of Garter in crown and tabard, and the signatures and appended seals of all three Kings of Arms are at the foot.
Bibliography: Wright, 1973, pp. 6. 27, Pl. 14.
BL Additional MS. 39249.

145 Coloured Woodcut Armorial Bookplate of Sir Nicholas Bacon, 1574.
153 × 100 mm.

The bookplate has the same arms, motto and crest as Sir Nicholas's Grant of Arms (no. 144). Below is this text: *N. Bacon eques auratus & magni sigilli Angliae Custos librum hunc bibliothecae Cantabrig. dicauit. 1574*. This is one of only ten surviving plates recording the bequest made by Bacon to aid the rebuilding of Cambridge University Library. It is the earliest known English printed bookplate.
Bibliography: E. R. Sandeen, 'The Origin of Sir Nicholas Bacon's Book-Plate', *Trans. Cambridge Bibl. Soc.*, 2 (1954–58), pp. 373–76.
BM P&D 1950–5–20–380.

146 Cup of Sir Nicholas Bacon, 1574.
Silver-gilt with the London hallmark for 1573–74, and a maker's mark; H 291 mm, D 174 mm.

The cup has a cover, almost hemispherical bowl, baluster stem and spreading foot. Around the lip of

145

146

the bowl is the legend · A · THYRDE · BOWLE · MADE · OF · THE · GREATE · SEALE · OF · ENGLANDE · AND · LEFT · BY · SYR · NYCHOLAS · BACON · KNYGT · LORDE · KEEPER · AS · AN · HEYRELOME · TO · HIS · HOWSE · OF · REDGRAVE · I · 5 · 7 · 4. From a band below this inscription are suspended three engraved shields of arms with strapwork surrounds: (1) Bacon (see no. 144); (2) Bacon impaling Ferneley (the arms of his wife's family); (3) Bacon differenced by a label of three points (for his son Nicholas), impaling Quarterly of 6: 1, Butts; 2, Bacon; 3, Buers; 4, Folliford (?); 5, Farmor; 6, Roydon. The cover has a pedestal supporting an urn surmounted by the Bacon crest of an ungilded ermine boar with a crescent on its left side. The pedestal also has the motto +MEDIOCRIA FIRMA. This cup was one of three made from the Great Seal of Philip and Mary, and bequeathed to each of Bacon's three houses, the others being Stiffkey (Norfolk) and Gorhambury (Herts.). Sir Nicholas Bacon was appointed Lord Keeper of the Great Seal on Elizabeth's accession, and as was customary, the seal of the preceding reign was broken up and presented to him. One of the other two cups is known to exist.
Bibliography: H. Read and A. B. Tonnochy, *Catalogue of the Silver Plate,* London (British Museum), 1928, no. 102, Pl. LX.
BM M&LA 1915, 3–13, 1. (Bequest of Mrs Edmond Wodehouse)

147 Seal Matrix of Sir Walter Raleigh (1552?–1618) as Governor of Virginia, 1584.
Silver; D 57 mm (hinged and pierced semi-circular handle on reverse).

The matrix bears the Raleigh arms (five fusils in a bend with a martlet for difference), crest and mantling, with two wolves as supporters; below is the motto AMORE · ET · VIRTVTE. Flanking the crest is the date 1584. The rim inscription reads: PROPRIA + TNSIHNIA [insignia] + WALTERI + RALEGH + MILITIS + DOMINI +& GVBERNATORIS + VIRGINAE + ETC. Sir Walter Raleigh was

renowned as a man of letters, soldier, sailor and explorer. He made repeated attempts to colonise Virginia, which ultimately ended in failure. He was executed by James I in 1618. This matrix is one of three belonging to Raleigh in the British Museum.
Bibliography: Tonnochy, 1952, no. 347.
BM M&LA 1904, 1–13, 2.

148 Illuminated Pedigree of the Hesketh Family, *c.* 1594.
Vellum; 450 × 525 mm.

An illuminated pedigree tracing the descent of the family of Hesketh of Rufford (Lancs.), and of related families, made in roll form but now mounted and bound as a book. The sixteenth century portion of the pedigree (there are continuations to the nineteenth century) is decorated with shields of arms and twenty-six half-length portraits. The date is given by reference to Sir Rowland Stanley 'now lyving 1594'. The last portrait in the roll shows Sir Robert Hesketh (d. 1620) flanked by his two wives. Sir Robert may have produced this illuminated roll as evidence during the heraldic visitation of Lancashire by Sir Richard St George, Clarenceux, in 1613, for it appears to be the source for Sir Richard's pedigree of Hesketh among the records of the visitation (Harley MS. 1427, ff. 124v.–125) with Sir Robert's signature at the foot.
Bibliography: Miscellanea Genealogica et Heraldica, ii (1876), pp. 140–49; Revd W. G. Procter, 'Notes on the Hesketh Pedigree', *Trans. Hist. Soc. Lancashire and Cheshire,* lxii (1911), pp. 58–66, and 6 plates; HCEC., no. 157, Pl. XLV; E. G. Millar, 'The Hesketh of Rufford Pedigree', *Brit. Mus. Quart.,* x (1935–6), p. 103, Pl. XXX.
BL Additional MS. 44026.

147

148 ▷

149 Finger-ring with the Arms of Fleetwood, sixteenth century.
Gold and crystal; D of hoop 27 mm.

The bezel bears the arms engraved on a crystal through which the tinctures, painted on foil, are visible (Per pale nebuly or and azure six martlets counter-changed). On the back of the bezel is engraved a grasshopper.

The ring was probably made for Sir William Fleetwood, Recorder of London (d. 1594).

Bibliography: Dalton, 1912, no. 319, Pl. V; W. J. Hemp, 'The Goodman and other grasshopper rings', *Ant. J.,* v (1925), pp. 406–407, Pl. XLIX, Fig. 4; Oman, 1974, p. 34, n. 11.

BM M&LA Franks Bequest No. 636.

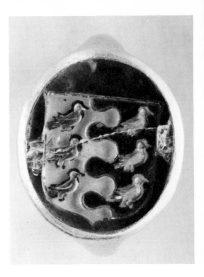

149

150 Finger-ring with the Arms of Tirrell, late sixteenth century.
Gold; D of hoop 30 mm.

The shield on the bezel bears two bars ermine between seven crosses formy and in chief a demi-lion issuant. Above are the initials IT, for Sir John Tirrell, knighted 1588.

Bibliography: Dalton, 1912, no. 600, Pl. VIII; Oman, 1974, p. 107, Pl. 48D.

BM M&LA Franks Bequest No. 810.

150

151 Finger-ring with the Arms of Corbet, late sixteenth–early seventeenth century.

Gold; D of hoop 26 mm.

The shield on the bezel bears Quarterly, 1, two ravens in pale within a bordure engrailed bezanty (Corbet); 2, two lions passant and a label of three points; 3, crusilly and two lions passant; 4, a fess and in chief a chevron.

Bibliography: Dalton, 1912, no. 616, Pl. IX; Oman, 1974, p. 107, Pl. 49 A.

BM M&LA Franks Bequest No. 826.

152 Seal Matrix of Richard Towneley (d. 1628).
Silver; D 53 mm (hinged and pierced semi-circular handle on reverse).

The matrix is engraved with a shield bearing the arms of Towneley (a fess and in chief three mullets) and seventeen other quarterings. The shield is enclosed in mantling and surmounted by three crests.

151

Hinged to the top of the handle is
a small oval matrix engraved with
a hawk holding a scroll bearing the
legend TENES · LE · VRAYE.
Bibliography: Tonnochy, 1952, no.
523.
BM M&LA 1927, 2–16, 45. (Gift of
Mill Stephenson)

**153 Seal Matrix of Charles Seton,
2nd Earl of Dunfermline** (d. 1672).
Silver; D 73 mm (hinged semi-
circular handle on reverse).

The matrix is engraved with a
shield of arms bearing Quarterly,
1 and 4, three crescents within a
double tressure flory counter-flory
(Seton); 2 and 3, on a fess three
cinquefoils (Hamilton). The shield
is surmounted by a coronet, crested
helmet and mantling, with two
horses as supporters. Legend:
SIGILLVM · CAROLI · SETONII ·
FERMELINODVNI · COMITIS · etc.
Charles Seton succeeded his father
as Earl in 1622 and the matrix
must have been made between then
and his death in 1672.
Bibliography: Tonnochy, 1952,
no. 782.
BM M&LA Franks Bequest No. 2880.

**154 Album with Arms of Frances,
Widow of the Duke of Richmond
and Lennox,** 1626.
Paper and vellum; 110 × 170 mm.

The signature, motto, and painted
arms of Frances, widow of the
Duke of Richmond and Lennox,
appear (ff. 16v.–17) in an *Album
amicorum* (i.e. 'album of friends')
kept by Charles Lewis, Elector
Palatine, son of Frederick V, King
of Bohemia, and Elizabeth, daughter
of James I. Entries in the album,
kept from 1622 to 1633, were
contributed by members of royal
and noble families and include
Charles I, Queen Henrietta Maria,
George Villiers, Duke of Buckingham,
and Charles Lewis's parents (his
father may have been the original
owner of the album). As in many
such albums the signatures are
accompanied by very fine paintings
of coats of arms, the work of
professional artists.
Bibliography: Nickson, 1970, p. 20.
BL Kings MS. 436.

152

155

155 Wine Bottle with the Arms of Allen, 1647.

Tin-glazed earthenware ('delft-ware'); H 153 mm.

Painted in blue with the word SACK (on the neck) and, below, the family arms (Ermine, on a chief three mullets), crest and mantling; inscribed: W^M ALLEN 1647. Made in London at Southwark.
Bibliography: Hobson, 1903, no. E20.
BM M&LA Franks Coll., 1887.

156 Bowl with the Arms of Packer, 1653.

Tin-glazed earthenware ('delft-ware'), with moulded lobed decoration on sides; D 285 mm, H 77 mm.

Painted in blue and yellow with the arms of Packer (a cross lozengy between four roses), with crest and mantling, and a set of initials and the date: P / A M 1653. Probably made in Southwark to commemorate a marriage by a member of the Packer family.
Bibliography: Hodgkin, 1891, no. 283; Hobson, 1903, no. E44; Amsterdam, 1973, no. 33.
BM M&LA 91, 5–24, 2.

157 Wine Bottle with the Arms of Hunlock(?), 1672.

Tin-glazed earthenware ('delftware'); H 170 mm.

Painted in blue and yellow with the family arms (Azure on a fess or three mullets of five points azure between three wolves' heads erased or), crest, helm and mantling; below the handle, the initial and the date: W 1672. Made in London, probably in Lambeth.
Bibliography: Hodgkin, 1891, no. 332; Hobson, 1903, no. E28.
BM M&LA Franks Coll., 1887.

158 Dish with the Arms of Treby, 1723.

Silver, with London hall-mark for 1723 and the mark of the goldsmith, Paul de Lamerie; D 610 mm.

The silver plaque emblazoned in high relief with the arms of the Rt Hon. George Treby, MP

158

Bibliography: Griggs, 1887, ill.
no. 5, 18; Tudor-Craig, 1925, p. 22.
BM OA 1887, 12–18, 44 (Franks
739+). (Revd C. H. Walker
Bequest)

**160 Coffee Pot with the Arms of
Clifford,** *c.* 1745.
Porcelain, decorated in gold,
grisaille and enamels; H 245 mm.

The pot bears the arms of Clifford
(Checky or and azure on a fess
gules a crescent argent for
difference) with crest and mantling.
It forms part of a service made in
China during the reign of the
Ch'ien-lung emperor (1736–95),
Ch'ing dynasty, for Hugh, 4th
Baron Clifford of Chudleigh
(1726–83).
Bibliography: Griggs, 1887, ill. no.
5, 3; Howard, 1974, pp. 297–98.
BM OA 1887, 12–18, 1 (Franks
816+). (Revd C. H. Walker
Bequest)

Colour plate

**161 Pair of Loving Cups with the
Arms of Banks,** *c.* 1760.
Porcelain, decorated in grisaille
and gilt; H 260 mm, D 150 mm.

The arms on each cup (a cross
between four fleurs-de-lis) and the
crest are taken from the bookplate
of Sir Joseph Banks (see no. 162).
The cups were made for him in
China during the reign of the
Ch'ien-lung emperor (1736–95),
Ch'ing dynasty. Sir Joseph Banks
(1743–1820) was a Knight of the
Bath and for forty-two years was
President of the Royal Society.
His collections and library are
preserved in the British Library.
Bibliography: Howard, 1974, p. 360.
BM OA 1887, 12–18, 7 (Franks
802+). (Revd C. H. Walker
Bequest)

**162 Engraved Armorial Bookplate
of Sir Joseph Banks** (1743–1820).
82 × 73 mm.

This bookplate provided the design
for the shields of arms on no. 161.
Bibliography: Book Plates Cat., i,
no. 1371.
BM P&D Bookplates no. 1371.

(Quarterly, 1 and 4, a lion rampant
with in chief three roundels; 2 and
3, party saltirewise, four griffins'
heads erased) is made separately
and applied to the centre of the
dish with screws and nuts. The
border combines gadrooning with
an intricate inner design against
a punched ground. This dish is an
early masterpiece in the *oeuvre* of
this leading Huguenot goldsmith.
Probably born in Holland in 1688,
while his parents were fleeing from
France *en route* for England, Paul
was apprenticed in 1703 to a
leading Huguenot *immigré* master,
Pierre Platel, and nine years later
entered his mark at Goldsmiths'
Hall. George Treby was one of his
influential patrons in the early years
of his career.
Bibliography: J. F. Hayward,
*Huguenot Silver in England, 1688–
1727*, London 1959, p. 45, Pls.
62–3; H. Tait, 'Huguenot silver
made in London (*c.* 1690–1723),
"The Peter Wilding Bequest",
Part 2', *The Connoisseur*, clxxxi
(1972), p. 33, Figs. 15–16.
BM M&LA 1969, 7–5, 25. (The
Peter Wilding Bequest)

**159 Plate with the Arms of Decker
impaling Watkins,** *c.* 1720.
Porcelain, decorated in underglaze
blue and 'famille verte' enamels;
D 322 mm.

The arms are Argent a demi-buck
gules, between his forelegs an
arrow vert in pale or, and on a
canton the Red Hand of Ulster (the
badge of a baronet), impaling
Azure a fess vair between three
leopards' heads jessant-de-lis or.
The plate is part of a service made
in China during the reign of the
K'ang-hsi emperor (1662–1722),
Ch'ing dynasty, for Sir Matthew
Decker (1679–1749).

163 Jug with the Arms of Chalmers, 1759.

Porcelain, painted with landscapes in colours (chiefly lilac) with gilding; H 149 mm.

Painted (on the front) is a shield with arms of Chalmers (Argent a demi-lion rampant sable issuing out of a fess gules with in base a fleur-de-lis gules), crest, mantling and motto: SPIRO; under the handle, a goose with a leaf in its bill on a crest wreath and, below, the initials and date: $\frac{A.C.}{1759}$. Made at Worcester and probably painted by James Rogers in 1759, perhaps for the Revd Alexander Chalmers, Minister of Cairnie (Aberdeenshire) and Chaplain to the 88th Regiment of Foot in 1759. He died in 1798.
Bibliography: Hobson, 1910, p. 82; Hobson, 1923, no. 386, Pl. 82; Marshall, 1946, pp. 190–91; H. Tait, 'James Rogers', *The Connoisseur*, cl (1962), p. 232, Fig. 17.
BM M&LA 1921, 12–15, 67.

164 Plate with the Arms of Gavin impaling Hearsey, *c.* 1765.

Porcelain, painted in colours, with gilding; D 226 mm.

Painted with the family arms (Argent a saltire sable and a sword piercing a mullet gules impaling Gules a chief argent), elaborate mantling and crest. Made for David Gavin, of Langton House (Berwickshire), who made a fortune as a tailor in Holland, where he married a Miss Hearsey, of Middelburg, Zeeland; he died in 1773. Worcester porcelain, but perhaps decorated in London at the workshop of James Giles.
Bibliography: Marshall, 1946, p. 198; Barrett, 1966, p. 52, Pl. 49A.
BM M&LA 1938, 3–14, 73.
(Wallace Elliot Bequest)

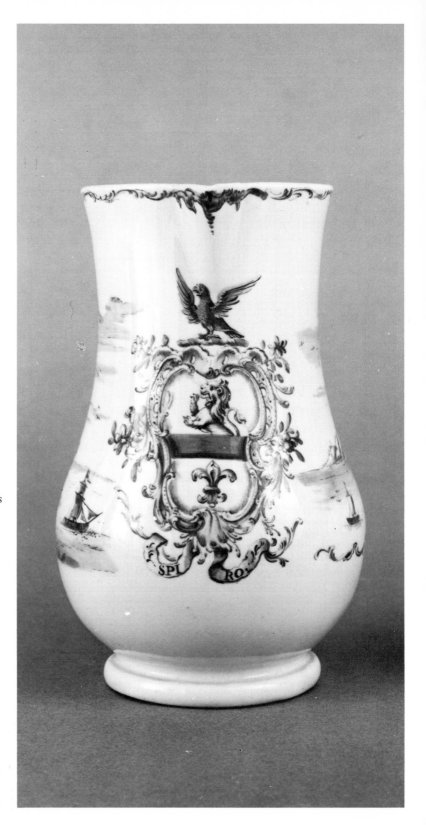

163

165 Teapot Stand with the Arms of Wilson impaling Langton, *c.* 1765.

Porcelain, with a blank transfer-printed shield and ribbon in black; details painted in colours subsequently; 127 × 143 mm.

The family arms (Argent a wolf rampant and on a chief three mullets impaling Per pale argent and purpure a cross moline gules overall a bend sable) and crest have incorrect tinctures, e.g. the field of the Wilson arms should be sable, not argent as on all extant pieces of this service. Made at Worcester about 1765 but perhaps decorated by an outside enameller.

Bibliography: Hobson, 1923, no. 376; Marshall, 1946, p. 194. BM M&LA 1923, 3–15, 148.

165

166 Tea Bowl and Saucer with the Arms of Burke impaling Nugent, 1774.
Porcelain, painted in colours, with gilding; H 42 mm (cup); D 125 mm (saucer).

Painted with the family arms (Or a cross gules in the dexter quarter a lion rampant sable impaling Ermine two bars gules), which are affixed to a pedestal surmounted by a putto-like figure of Hymen holding a torch, and, on either side, emblematic figures of Liberty and Plenty; below, a Latin inscription:

I. BVRKE. OPT. B. M.
R. ET. I. CHAMPION D. D. D.
PIGNUS AMICITIAE
III. NON. NOV. MDCCLXXIV

(Translated: 'R. and J. Champion gave this as a token of their friendship to J. Burke, the best of British wives on 3rd day of November, 1774'). Part of the most famous and extravagantly painted of all British porcelain services, that given to Jane, wife of Edmund Burke, the Whig MP for Bristol 1774–80, as a joint present from the new proprietor of the Bristol porcelain factory and his wife, Judith.
Bibliography: H. Owen, *Two Centuries of Ceramic Art in Bristol,* London, 1873, pp. 96–97, Pl. VI; Bristol, 1970, no. 78d.
BM M&LA 1913, 12–20, 159.
(Revd A. H. S. Barwell Bequest)

167 Plaque with the Arms of Richard Champion, 1774–78.
Porcelain, biscuit (unglazed) oval plaque with chaplet of flowers in high relief; 180 × 148 mm (inc. wooden frame).

In centre, painted on a small glazed medallion are the arms of Richard Champion (Argent on a fess sable a phoenix displayed argent, between three trefoils slipped vert, all within a bordure gules bezanty or), to whom had been transferred on 6 May 1774 the famous patent of William Cookworthy (1768) for the manufacture of true ('hard-paste') porcelain and who continued to run the Bristol factory until its closure in 1781.
Bibliography: F. Hurlbutt, *Bristol*

Porcelain, London and Boston, 1928, p. 98, pl. 61; A. J. Toppin, 'A Bristol plaque with the Arms of Champion', *Trans. English Ceramic Circle,* 1, pt. 2 (1934), p. 41; Bristol, 1970, no. 55.
BM M&LA 1938, 3–14, 81.
(Wallace Elliot Bequest)

168 Plate with the Arms of Honeywood impaling Courtenay, probably 1778.
Cream-coloured earthenware, painted in colours, with gilding; on reverse, impressed mark: WEDGWOOD E2; D 249 mm.

Painted with the Honeywood arms (Argent a chevron between three eagles' heads erased azure with an escutcheon bearing the Red Hand of Ulster) impaling those of Courtenay (Quarterly, 1 and 4, Or three roundels gules, 2 and 3, Or a lion rampant azure) in a roundel in the centre; on the rim, a decorative border incorporating the crest. Made at Wedgwood's factory in Staffordshire but probably

decorated outside, perhaps in London by Abbot (see no. 169); presumably completed about the time of the marriage of Sir John Honeywood, Bt. to Frances, eldest daughter of William, 2nd Viscount Courtenay, in 1778.
Bibliography: Hobson, 1903, no. I.788; H. Tait, 'The Wedgwood Collection in the British Museum', *Proc. Wedgwood Soc.,* No. 4 (1961), pp. 196–97, Pl. 25C.
BM M&LA Franks Coll., 1887.

169 Soup Plate with the Arms of Giffard impaling Courtenay, probably 1788.
Cream-coloured earthenware, painted in colours, with gilding; on reverse, impressed mark: TURNER 3; D 248 mm.

The roundel in the centre has the Giffard arms (Azure three stirrups with leathers or) impaling those of Courtenay (see no. 168); on the rim, a decorative border incorporating the crest. Made at Turner's factory in Staffordshire but probably

168

decorated in London at 82 Fleet Street, where 'Turner and Abbot', according to an advertisement dated 31 January 1785, had established a 'Manufactory for enamelling . . . and will engage to finish a service of Ware to any Pattern, in the course of three or four days after the order is given, either with Crests, Cyphers, or Borders'. Part of a service (now dispersed) presumed to have been completed about the time of the marriage of Thomas Giffard, of Chillington (Staffs.), to Charlotte, second daughter of William, 2nd Viscount Courtenay, on 23 June, 1788.
Bibliography: Hobson, 1903, no. K20, Pl. XXXVII; *Trans. English Ceramic Circle*, 4, pt. 5 (1959), pp. 58–59; B. Hillier, *Master Potters of the Industrial Revolution, The Turners of Lane End*, London, 1965, pp. 55–62.
BM M&LA 96, 4–10, 1. (Gift of Mr John Tolhurst)

170 Dish with the Arms of Bostock with Rich in pretence, 1783–90.
Porcelain, painted in colours, with gilding, in the form of a square dessert dish; 238 × 237 mm.

Painted within a wreath of flowers in the centre is a shield of arms (Sable a fess humetty argent with on an escutcheon Gules a chevron between three crosses patonce or). Made at Worcester for the Revd Charles Bostock, of Ross Hall (Suffolk), who married in 1783 the heiress of Lieut.-General Sir Robert Rich, of Ross Hall and assumed by royal licence (dated 28 December 1790) the name of Rich; created a Baronet as Sir Charles Rich on 28 July 1791. The shield is an example of the reversion to medieval forms which took place during the Gothic Revival.
Bibliography: Hobson, 1923, no. 389, Pl. 83; Marshall, 1946, p. 205.
BM M&LA 1923, 3–15, 147.

171 Cup and Saucer with Arms of Lord Nelson, 1802.
Porcelain, painted in colours, with gilding; H 60 mm (cup); D 158 mm (saucer).

Painted with a border of oak leaves and, in the centre, the arms of Lord Nelson (Or a cross patonce sable, a bend gules surmounted by another engrailed of the field, charged with three bombs fired proper; on a chief undulating argent waves of the sea, from which a palm tree, issuant between a disabled ship on the dexter and a battery in ruins on the sinister; over the palm is a crescent gules) encircled by the motto of the Order of the Bath, with two crests, supporters, motto and (?) foreign order. Part of a service made at Robert Chamberlain's factory in Worcester, shortly after Lord and Lady Nelson's visit in 1802.
Bibliography: Hobson, 1910, p. 149; Barrett, 1966, p. 63.
BM M&LA 1928, 1–16, 2. (Given by Mrs Garwood)

171

(i)   (ii)   (iii)

(iv)   (v)   (vi)

(vii)   (viii)   (ix)

(x)   (xi)   (xii)

VI
Royal Heraldry

The Royal arms are the most frequently displayed of all heraldic achievements. It is impossible here to give more than an indication of the vast range of items which bear them. The evolution of the Royal arms over the centuries is demonstrated here primarily by coins and seals, with a few pieces included to show their occurrence in manuscripts, glass, ceramics and textiles. No. 227 is an example of how artists and craftsmen have sometimes mis-represented the Royal arms. A number of items also illustrate the changes that have taken place in the supporters used for the Royal arms, display the armorial bearings of Queen consorts and provide examples of differencing used to denote the princes of the blood royal.

The Royal arms of England have undergone many alterations, reflecting both historical changes affecting the monarchy and the developments in heraldic practice.

The earliest known representation of the arms of the Kingdom of England (Gules three lions passant guardant or) is on the shield borne by the equestrian figure of King Richard I on his second Great Seal, dated 1198 (no. 205). Matthew Paris attributed these arms to all the English Kings from William the Conqueror until Richard, but this was an anachronism, just as the armorial bearings invented in the late Middle Ages for legendary and renowned pre-Conquest monarchs, such as Edward the Confessor's Azure a cross patonce between five martlets or (no. 203) are fictitious. There are some vague allusions in literary sources which suggest the possibility that Richard's father, Henry II, bore Gules a lion rampant or. Richard's first Great Seal of 1189 has what appears to be a single lion rampant (no. 204), and this gives some substance to the literary evidence. The 1177 seal of Richard's brother John (later King John) as Lord of Ireland and Count of Mortain is known to have had a shield bearing two lions passant guardant and it is possible that the arms on Richard's second Great Seal derived from this.

Whatever the origin of these arms, they remained those of the Kings of England down to 1340 (nos. 172, 207, 208). In this year, Edward III, having renewed his claim to the French throne, quartered the arms of the Kingdom of France (Azure semé with fleurs-de-lis or) with those of England (nos. 173, 210). Richard II and, for the opening years of his reign, Henry IV, used the same arms. During the first decade of the fifteenth century, the French quartering was altered to Azure three fleurs-de-lis or, and since then the two versions have been known as France ancient and France modern (no. 176). The precise date at which this change was first made is still not clear. The new arms of France quartered with England occur on Henry IV's second Great Seal, which came into use during November 1406, but there is some evidence to suggest that certain of the royal princes had adopted these arms a few years earlier.

France modern quartered with England remained the arms of the royal Houses of Plantagenet and Tudor down to the death of Elizabeth I in 1603 (nos. 177–186). For a brief period, between 1554 and 1558, these arms were sometimes impaled with those of Spain to denote the joint reign of Queen Mary I and her husband Philip of Spain. This shield occurs on the silver coinage of the period (no. 185) and on the Great Seal of the reign.

The accession of James VI of Scotland to the English throne in 1603 as James I resulted in extensive alterations to the Royal arms. The French and English quartered arms were placed in the first and fourth quarters, and the arms of the Kingdom of Scotland (Or a lion rampant within a double-tressure flory counter-flory gules) were introduced into the second quarter; the arms of Ireland (Azure a harp or stringed argent), representing the hereditary title of King of Ireland, granted to Henry VIII in 1541, filled the third quarter (no. 187).

This shield was used by James I, Charles I, Charles II and James II, with an interruption during the Commonwealth and Protectorate, when the Royal arms were abolished. Instead, the coinage and seals of the Commonwealth have shields bearing the cross of St George and the harp of Ireland, placed side by side (nos. 189, 226). In 1655 a new Great Seal was struck, both sides of which have the arms of Oliver Cromwell as Lord Protector of England, Scotland and Ireland: Quarterly 1 and 4, Argent a cross gules (St George of England); 2, Azure a saltire argent (St Andrew, for Scotland); 3, Azure a harp or stringed argent (Ireland), with an escutcheon of pretence bearing the Cromwell arms of Sable a lion rampant argent (no. 190). The same arms were used by Cromwell's son Richard, but at the Restoration in 1660 the Stuart Royal arms were re-adopted.

Following the flight of James II in 1688 and his replacement on the English throne by his daughter Mary II and her husband William III of Orange, the Royal arms were modified three times before the end of their joint reign. William and Mary's first shield of arms took account of the fact that the Scottish parliament did not recognize them as sovereigns of their country until April, 1689. From the 1688 Revolution until then, the Royal arms consisted of Quarterly 1 and 4, France modern quartering England, 2 and 3, Ireland, with an escutcheon overall bearing Azure billety and a lion rampant or (Nassau, for William III). In April 1689, following the recognition by the Scots of William and Mary, the arms were altered to incorporate the Kingdom of Scotland. The resulting shield bore Quarterly, 1, England; 2, Scotland; 3, Ireland; 4, France modern, with an escutcheon of Nassau overall. This shield appears briefly on half-crowns issued in that year (no. 193), but was superseded within a few months by a reversion to the Royal arms as used by the Stuarts from 1603, with the addition of the Nassau escutcheon (no. 194). This shield remained as the Royal arms after Mary's death in 1694. On Queen Anne's accession in 1702, the Nassau escutcheon was dropped. The 1707 Act of Union between England and Scotland caused another change. The arms of England and Scotland were impaled in the first and fourth quarters, France modern was placed in the second quarter and Ireland remained in the third (no. 196).

These arms continued for the remaining seven years of Anne's reign. The accession in 1714 of the Elector of Hanover as King George I resulted in the replacement in the fourth quarter of the impaled England and Scotland arms by those of Hanover: Tierced per pale and per chevron; 1, Gules two lions passant guardant or (Brunswick), 2, Or semé of hearts gules, a lion rampant azure (Luneburg), 3, Gules a horse courant argent (Westphalia), overall an escutcheon gules charged with the crown of Charlemagne or (the Arch-treasureship of the Holy Roman Empire) (no. 197).

The next change in the Royal arms took place in 1801 when, on the Union with Ireland, the French arms (and George III's title of King of France) were omitted, the arms of England placed in the first and fourth quarters, Scotland in the second and Ireland in the third, with the arms of Hanover placed on an escutcheon overall surmounted by the electoral bonnet (no. 199). In 1816, as a result of the elevation of the Electorate of Hanover into a Kingdom, a royal crown replaced the bonnet (no. 200). The final alteration to the Royal arms occurred on Queen Victoria's accession in 1837. Because of her sex she was unable to succeed to the throne of Hanover as well as England, so the Hanoverian escutcheon and crown were removed. From this date the Royal arms of England have remained unchanged (no. 202).

Select Bibliography

Heenan, M. G., 'The French Quartering in the Arms of King Henry IV', *The Coat of Arms*, x (1968–69), pp. 215–21.

——, and Humphery-Smith, C. R., 'The Royal Heraldry of England', *The Coat of Arms*, vi (1960–61), pp. 224–28, 308–9; vii (1962–63), pp. 18–24, 30–34, 122–27, 164–69, 213–16, 254–58, 321–24.

Petchey, W. J., *Armorial Bearings of the Sovereigns of England*, Standing Conference for Local History, 2nd ed., revised, London, 1977.

172 Pendant with the pre-1340 Arms of England, late thirteenth or fourteenth century.
Enamelled bronze; H 45 mm.

This shield-shaped pendant bears three lions passant guardant against a red enamelled background (the arms of England before the quartering with France in 1340). The red enamel is well preserved and the lions retain traces of gilding. The presence of the Royal arms suggests that it might have decorated the horse harness of a royal official.
BM M&LA 88, 6–8, 8. (Gift of A. W. Franks)

173 Gold Noble of Edward III, 1351.
Pre-Treaty Coinage, series B. London mint.

The obverse shows the King in a ship holding a shield charged with Quarterly France ancient and England.
Bibliography: L. A. Lawrence, *The coinage of Edward III from 1351,* Oxford, 1937.
BM C&M 1935–1–1–7. (Gift of L. A. Lawrence)

174 Gold Quarter-Noble of Richard II, *c.* 1380.
Type I. London mint.

The obverse shows a shield bearing Quarterly France ancient and England.
Bibliography: F. A. Walters, 'The coinage of Richard II', *Numis. Chron.,* (1904), pp. 326–52.
BM C&M 1920–8–16–41. (Gift of the Goldsmiths' Company)

175 Gold Noble of Henry IV, *c.* 1400.
Heavy Coinage, type Ia. London mint.

The obverse shows the King in a ship holding a shield with Quarterly France ancient and England.
Bibliography: Blunt, 1941–3, pp. 22–27.
BM C&M 1898–3–1–35.

176 Gold Noble of Henry IV, *c.* 1405.

Heavy Coinage, type Ib. London mint.

The obverse shows the King in a ship holding a shield charged with Quarterly France modern and England.
Bibliography: Blunt, 1941–3, pp. 22–27.
BM C&M 1909–6–10–8.

177 Gold Half-Noble of Henry V, *c.* 1420.
Type F/E. London mint.

The obverse shows the King in a ship holding a shield charged with Quarterly France modern and England.
Bibliography: G. C. Brooke, 'The privy-marks of Henry V', *Numis. Chron.,* (1930), pp. 44–47, and *idem., English Coins,* 3rd ed., London, 1950, p. 144.
BM C&M 1915–5–7–584.

178 Gold Angelot of Henry VI, *c.* 1445.
Rouen mint, fourth issue.

The obverse shows an angel holding the shields of the kingdoms of France and England.
The Angelot (or $\frac{2}{3}$ Salute) was part of the series of coins struck at French mints for Henry VI as king of France. The placing of shields side by side to denote two states ruled by one dynasty was first used on coins by Philip the Good, Duke of Burgundy, for the coins of his possessions in the Low Countries.
Bibliography: L. C. Hewlitt, *Anglo-Gallic Coins,* London, 1920, pp. 211, 234–36.
BM C&M 1843–12–14–4.

179 Gold Ryal of Edward IV, 1465–66.
London mint.

The obverse (type V) shows a rose on the side of a ship, a banner with the King's initial E and a shield bearing Quarterly France modern and England. The reverse (type VI) shows a rose *en soleil.*
It is at this period that the King's personal badges, here the sun and rose, first appear regularly on the coinage as part of the type or

among the devices known as initial marks which are placed at the beginning of the obverse and/or reverse legends to denote the different periods of coinage.
Bibliography: C. E. Blunt and C. A. Whitton, 'The Coinage of Edward IV and Henry VI (Restored)', *Brit. Numis. J.,* xxv (1945–8), pp. 130–82.
BM C&M 1935–6–3–15 and 1935–4–1–6392. (Gift of L. A. Lawrence and T. B. Clarke-Thornhill Bequest)

180 Gold Angel of Richard III, 1483–85.
Initial mark: sun and rose dimidiated. London mint.

The reverse retains the ship of the Noble type but the armed figure of the King is replaced by a cross supported below by a shield bearing Quarterly France modern and England and on either side by the King's initial and the Yorkist rose. The Angel was introduced alongside the Ryal in 1465 and by 1483 had superseded it as the standard English gold coin. It remained the principal medium of large-scale commerce throughout the following Tudor period.
Bibliography: E. J. Winstanley, 'The angels and groats of Richard III', *Brit. Numis. J.,* xxiv (1941–4), pp. 179–86.
BM C&M 1935–4–1–388.

181 Gold Double Sovereign of Henry VII, *c.* 1504–9.
Initial mark: arrow. London mint.

The reverse shows a shield bearing Quarterly France modern and England in the centre of a Tudor rose.
First ordered by Henry VII in 1489, the Sovereign was essentially a prestige coin whose splendour was intended to rival the gold *grote reaal* of the Burgundian Netherlands, introduced two years previously by the Emperor Maximilian I, from whose types the earliest English Sovereign was derived.
Bibliography: W. J. W. Potter and

E. J. Winstanley, 'The coinage of Henry VII', *Brit. Numis. J.*, xxxii (1963), pp. 140–60; P. Grierson, 'The origins of the English sovereign and the symbolism of the closed crown', *Brit. Numis. J.*, xxxiii (1964), pp. 118–34.
BM C&M 1866–7–13–1.

182 Gold Crown of Henry VIII, 1526–29.
Second Coinage, initial mark: rose. London mint.

The reverse shows a crowned shield bearing Quarterly France modern and England. The design followed that of the contemporary French *écu* with which the English Crown also conformed in weight and fineness.
Bibliography: Whitton, 1949–51, pp. 171–82.
BM C&M 1935–4–1–933. (T. B. Clarke-Thornhill Bequest)

183 Gold Sovereign of Henry VIII, 1545–47.
Third Coinage, initial mark: S. Southwark mint.

The reverse shows a crowned shield bearing Quarterly France modern and England with lion and dragon supporters and the King's monogram below.
Bibliography: Whitton, 1949–51, pp. 67–80.
BM C&M E 0005.

184 Silver Crown of Edward VI, 1551.
Third period, initial mark: Y. London mint.

The obverse shows the first mounted figure of a king to appear on an English coin. The Tudor rose appears on the trappers of the horse.
Bibliography: H. W. Morrieson, 'The silver coins of Edward VI', *Brit. Numis. J.*, xii (1915), pp. 165–79.
BM C&M 1935–4–1–1823. (T. B. Clarke-Thornhill Bequest)

185 Silver Shilling of Philip and Mary, 1554.
Undated issue, English and Spanish titles. London mint.

The reverse shows an oval shield with the arms of Spain impaling the Royal arms of England.
Bibliography: H. Symonds, 'The coinage of Queen Mary Tudor', *Brit. Numis. J.*, viii (1911), pp. 179–201.
BM C&M 1850–6–1–66.

186 Gold Pound Sovereign of Elizabeth I, 1594–96.
Initial mark: woolpack. London mint.

The obverse shows a half-length profile portrait of the Queen. On the reverse is a crowned shield bearing Quarterly France modern and England with ER on either side.
Bibliography: H. Symonds, 'The mint of Elizabeth I', *Numis. Chron.*, (1916) pp. 61–105.
BM C&M 1937–11–12–1 and 1864–7–13–27. (The first example given by the Brooke family in memory of A. Brooke)

187 Gold Unite of James I, 1603–4.
First Coinage, initial mark: thistle.

The reverse shows the first use on an English coin of the Stuart Royal arms (Quarterly, 1 and 4, France and England; 2, Scotland; 3, Ireland) with IR on either side.
Bibliography: H. Symonds, 'Mint marks and denominations of the coinage of James I', *Brit. Numis. J.*, ix (1912), pp. 207–27.
BM C&M 1935–4–1–6822. (T. B. Clarke-Thornhill Bequest)

188 Gold Angel of Charles I, 1625–26.
Initial mark: cross calvary. London mint.

The reverse shows the modified Angel type, introduced in 1619–20 for James I, on which a more realistic ship displays the Stuart Royal arms on its sail. After 1603 the fine gold Angel was gradually superseded by the slightly baser Unite as the standard English commercial gold coin, but small quantities of Angels continued to be struck during the reign of Charles I principally for ceremonial purposes such as the ceremony of touching for the king's evil.
Bibliography: H. Farquhar, 'Royal Charities, part I. Angels as healing pieces for the king's evil', *Brit. Numis. J.*, xi (1914), pp. 39–135.
BM C&M P 147 N 73.

189 Gold Unite of the Commonwealth, 1649.
London mint.

The reverse shows the conjoined shields of the cross of St George for England and the harp for Ireland. This coinage of the English parliament omits the arms of Scotland. The shape of the arms on the Commonwealth coinage led to its being nicknamed 'breeches money' which was, as Lord Lucas said, 'a fit stamp for the coin of the rump'.
BM C&M 1935–4–1–7841. (T. B. Clarke-Thornhill Bequest)

190 Medal Commemorating Cromwell's Elevation to the Protectorate, 1653.
Gold; D 38mm.

On the reverse is a lion sejant, laureate, holding the shield of Cromwell as Lord Protector (Quarterly, 1 and 4, the cross of St George; 2, the cross of St Andrew; 3, the harp of Ireland, with the paternal arms of Cromwell, a lion rampant, on an escutcheon).
Legend: PAX · QVAERITVR · BELLO. The obverse has a bust of Cromwell. The medal was commissioned from Thomas Simon, Chief Engraver to the Mint, by Cromwell.
Bibliography: *Medallic Ill.*, i, no. 45, pp. 409–10.
BM C&M M7364.

191 Gold Five Guineas of Charles II, 1668.
London mint, designed and engraved by John Roettier.

The reverse shows the crowned shields of England, Scotland, France and Ireland arranged cross-fashion with four interlaced Cs in the centre and, in the angles, four sceptres with orb, thistle, lis and harp heads symbolising the countries over which the King had, or claimed, dominion.
This is the first appearance on the coinage of the cruciform arrangement of the Royal arms which was

to be frequently revived, with appropriate modifications, until the twentieth century. It made its most recent appearance on the 1960 Crown piece of Elizabeth II.
BM C&M VI P. 75 N 200.

192 Gold Five Guineas of James II, 1686.
London mint, designed and engraved by John Roettier.

The reverse is similar to that of no. 191 but with the central initials omitted.
BM C&M 1946–10–4–651. (Oldroyd Bequest)

193 Silver Half-Crown of William and Mary, 1689.
London mint, designed and engraved by James Roettier.

The reverse shows the form of Royal arms introduced briefly from 11 April 1689, following the Scots' recognition of the joint monarchy: Quarterly, 1, England; 2, Scotland; 3, Ireland; 4, France, with an escutcheon with the arms of Nassau overall.
BM C&M 1919–9–18–199. (Gift of T. H. B. Graham)

194 Silver Half-Crown of William and Mary, 1689.
London mint, designed and engraved by James Roettier.

The reverse shows the form of Royal arms which replaced that shown on no. 193 before the end of 1689 and which remained standard during the rest of the reign and later for William III alone. The arms are the usual Stuart form with the escutcheon of Nassau overall.
BM C&M 1919–9–18–203. (Gift of T. H. B. Graham)

195 Silver Crown of Anne, 1707.
London mint, designed and engraved by John Croker.

The reverse shows the crowned shields of England, Scotland, France and Ireland arranged cross-fashion in the form used before the Act of Union. Between the arms are roses and the feathers of the Prince of Wales.
BM C&M 1919–9–18–332. (Gift of T. H. B. Graham)

196 Silver Crown of Anne, 1707.
London mint, designed and engraved by John Croker or Samuel Bull (under-engraver).

The reverse shows two crowned shields of England and Scotland impaled and the shields of Ireland and France arranged cross-fashion in the form used after the Act of Union.
BM C&M 1919–9–18–333. (Gift of T. H. B. Graham)

197 Gold Five Guineas of George I, 1716.
London mint, designed and engraved by Johann Rudolph Ochs, Senior.

The reverse shows the modification and rearrangement of the traditional cruciform pattern of crowned shields necessitated by the accession of the Elector of Hanover to the British throne. The second shield of England and Scotland impaled has been dropped and the shield of Hanover inserted at the left-hand arm of the cross.
BM C&M 1810 E 1882.

198 Gold Five Guineas of George II, 1729.
London mint, designed and engraved by Johann Sigismund Tanner.

The reverse shows a crowned shield bearing Quarterly, 1, England and Scotland; 2, France; 3, Ireland; 4, Hanover.
BM C&M 1829 E 1927.

199 Silver Pattern Dollar Bank Token of George III, 1804.
London mint, designed and engraved by Conrad Heinrich Küchler.

The reverse shows a crowned shield within the Garter bearing the Royal arms: Quarterly, 1 and 4, England; 2, Scotland; 3, Ireland, and an escutcheon of Hanover overall surmounted by an electoral bonnet. This form of the Royal arms first appears on the coinage on the half-guineas of 1801. During this period of acute silver shortage, bullion from stocks in the Bank of England was struck into silver tokens. This design was never in fact used for currency purposes.

Bibliography: Linecar and Stone, 1968, p. 25.
BM C&M 1926–8–17–720. (Gift of Ruth Weightman)

200 Gold Pattern Two Pounds of George IV, 1826.
London mint, designed and engraved by Jean Baptiste Meslen.

The reverse shows a crowned and mantelled shield, with the same arms as no. 199 except that the electoral bonnet is replaced by a crown.
These two pounds were not issued for circulation, but the same design was used for currency Sovereigns.
BM C&M 1946–10–4–662. (Oldroyd Bequest)

201 Gold Proof Two Pounds of William IV, 1831.
London mint, designed and engraved by Jean Baptiste Meslen.

The reverse shows a crowned and mantelled shield similar to the previous coin but further elaborated by the addition of the Garter collar and by hatching to indicate the heraldic colours present in the quarterings.
BM C&M E 3579a.

202 Silver Proof Crown of Victoria, 1847.
London mint, 'Gothic' type, designed by William Dyce and engraved by William Wyon.

The reverse shows the four crowned shields of England (twice), Scotland and Ireland arranged cross-fashion with the Garter star in the centre and the floral symbols of the three parts of the United Kingdom in the angles, within a cusped border. Although several thousand 'Gothic' crowns were struck, they were not produced for general circulation, but a similar design for the florin was used for currency pieces.
Bibliography: Linecar and Stone, 1968, pp. 88–89.
BM C&M 1919–9–18–609. (Gift of T. H. B. Graham)

203

203 Inlaid Tile with the Arms of Edward the Confessor,
mid-fifteenth century.
W 140 mm.

This corner tile of a sixteen-tile pattern is from Great Malvern Priory (Worcs.). The fictitious arms assigned to Edward the Confessor (a cross patonce between five martlets) were adopted by Westminster Abbey, the resting place of his relics. Malvern Priory was originally a cell of Westminster Abbey and this explains the repeated occurrence of the arms on Malvern tiles. The full sixteen-tile pattern exists in the pavement of Abbot Sebroke in Gloucester Cathedral dated 1455.
Bibliography: E. Eames, 'The Canynges Pavement', *J. Brit. Arch. Assoc.*, xiv (1951), pp. 33–46.
BM M&LA tile no. 3143.

204 First Great Seal of Richard I,
1189–98.
Green wax; D 102 mm.

The King is shown armed and mounted with a shield bearing a lion rampant (reverse). The sharply curved shield presents only one half of its surface to view, so that the complete device may be two lions rampant combatant. The obverse shows the King enthroned.
Bibliography: Birch, i, no. 81; Landon, 1935, pp. 173–83.
BL Seal no. xxxix.11.

205 Second Great Seal of Richard I,
1198.
Green wax; D 99 mm.

The armed and mounted King bears a shield with three lions passant guardant (reverse). This second Great Seal was cut in 1195 after Richard's return from captivity during the Third Crusade. It was brought into use in 1198, and since then the three lions passant guardant have remained the Royal arms of England. The obverse shows the King enthroned.

Bibliography: Birch, i, no. 87; Landon, 1935, pp. 173–83.
BL Cotton Charter XVI. 1.

206 Great Seal of King Edward I,
1276.
Dark green wax; D 110 mm.

The King is shown mounted in armour with the lions of England on his shield and horse-trapper (reverse). The obverse shows the King enthroned.
Bibliography: Birch, i, no. 132.
BL Seal no. xliii. 142.

207 Inlaid Tile with the pre-1340 Arms of England, late thirteenth or early fourteenth century.
W 137 mm.

This tile, bearing the three lions passant guardant arms of England, was found in an unspecified churchyard in Somerset.
BM M&LA tile no. 682.

208 Double Matrix of the Seal for the Delivery of Wool and Hides, Lincoln, early fourteenth century.
Bronze; D 48·5 mm (circular, with four loops and pegs).

The obverse bears the pre-1340 Royal arms of England on a shield suspended by a strap and flanked by two birds, the reverse just the Royal arms.
Bibliography: Tonnochy, 1952, no. 39.
BM M&LA 56, 4–28, 1 (reverse), 1842 No. 8 (obverse). (Gifts of Mrs Piggott and the Lords of the Treasury)

209 Walter de Milemete's Treatise for King Edward III, *c.* 1326–27.
Vellum; 238 × 154 mm.

Illuminated manuscript copy of the treatise '*De Secretis Secretorum*', a popular pseudo-Aristotelian work on the education and duties of princes. The lavish heraldic ornamentation in the borders and miniatures forms an Illustrative roll of Royal arms. On the exhibited pages (ff. 16v.–17) the arms of England for Edward II appear on shields in the lower borders, on the robe of the King in the miniature (f. 16), and on the

210

surcoat of the border figure
of a knight in mail (f. 17).
Shields for Edward III as Earl of
Chester (England with a label of five
points azure) and for Henry, 3rd
Earl of Lancaster, d. 1345 (England
with a baston azure), demonstrate
forms of differencing.
According to the preface of a
companion MS. in Christ Church
Library, Oxford, the treatise was
transcribed for presentation to
Edward III by Walter de Milemete.
Bibliography: M. R. James, *The
Treatise of Walter de Milemete*,
Roxburghe Club, 1913; T. C. Skeat,
'Manuscripts and Printed Books
from Holkham Hall Library', *Brit.
Mus. Quart.*, xvii (1952), pp. 23–33,
Pl. X.
BL Additional MS. 47680.

**210 Sixth Great Seal of King
Edward III**, 1340–72.
Green wax; D 115 mm.

The King is shown enthroned
accompanied by two seated lions
beneath a Gothic triple canopy; on
either side is a shield of arms of
Quarterly France ancient and
England (obverse). The reverse
shows the King mounted in armour
with the same arms on his shield
and horse-trapper.
Bibliography: Birch, i, no. 186.
BL Seal no. xxxvi. 4.

**211 Seal of Anne of Bohemia,
Wife of King Richard II**, 1390.
Red wax; D 60 mm.

The shield of arms bears the Royal
arms of England impaling those of
the German Empire quartering
Bohemia. The arms of Anne of
Bohemia in a different quartering
appear on the exhibited pages of
Nicholas Upton's treatise (no. 33).
Bibliography: Birch, i, no. 804.
BL Additional Charter 20396.

**212 Select Psalms of Humphrey,
Duke of Gloucester** (d. 1447),
c. 1440.
Vellum; 242 × 165 mm.

The initial S on f. 7 contains the
arms of Duke Humphrey (Quarterly
France modern and England
differenced by a bordure argent); at
the base of the page is a shield of
the same arms supported by two
antelopes sejant argent, ducally
gorged or and surmounted by a
helmet and crest (on a chapeau
gules turned up ermine a crowned
lion statant guardant or). Duke
Humphrey, fourth son of Henry V,
was the first important patron in
England to show an interest in
Italian humanistic studies. This is
reflected in the illumination of this
manuscript, for although it was
executed by an English artist (to
whom has also been attributed no.
111), in the borders on some folios
he copied the white-vine ornament
of Italian humanist manuscripts. On
f. 8 (not shown) is a miniature
depicting Duke Humphrey presented
by St Alban to the Man of Sorrows.
Bibliography: British Museum,
*Reproductions from Illuminated
Manuscripts*, Series I, 1907, Pl. XVII;
Oxford, Bodleian Library exhib.
cat., *Duke Humfrey and English
Humanism in the Fifteenth
Century*, 1970, no. 8A; Alexander,
1972, p. 169.
BL Royal MS. 2 B. i.

**213 Inlaid Tile with the Arms of
England and France**, mid-fifteenth
century.
H 220 mm.

The tile bears Quarterly France
modern and England. It was part
of a series of five wall tiles (see
also no. 126), the topmost tile of
which has the date 36 Henry VI
(1457–58).
From Great Malvern Priory (Worcs.).
Bibliography: Hobson, 1903, no.
A 262; Eames, 1968, Colour
Plate C.
BM M&LA tile no. 1332.

**214 Sword of State of the Prince of
Wales**, fifteenth century.
H 1·810 m.

212

This Sword of State was carried before the Prince of Wales since it bears on the principal side of the grip and pommel the following arms:

1) Quarterly France modern and England supported by angels and with a crown above;
2) Or three lions passant guardant gules, for the Kings of Wales;
3) Sable bezanty, for Cornwall;
4) On the pommel Argent a cross gules (St George).

On the outer side there are: 1) Mortimer quartering Burgh; 2) Chester; 3) Argent a chief azure. The quillons and sides of the hilt have defaced inscriptions in Dutch or Low German. These suggest that the sword was probably made in Holland or North Germany in the second half of the fifteenth century. The enamelled arms were presumably inserted after it had been brought to England. The sword may have been used by Prince Edward, eldest son of Edward IV. He was made Duke of Cornwall at birth and in 1471 was created Prince of Wales and Earl of Chester. The sword may have been borne before him in 1475 when he 'came to Chester in great pompe'. In 1483 he succeeded his father as King Edward V, but was imprisoned in the Tower of London with his younger brother and appears to have died in the reign of his uncle, Richard III. Alternatively, it may have been used by Prince Edward (1473–84), son of Richard III, who was invested as Prince of Wales and Earl of Chester at York in September 1483.

Bibliography: R. Gough, *Sepulchral Monuments in Great Britain*, i, pt. 1, London, 1786, p. 148; *Vetusta Monumenta*, London, 1835, v, Pl. 50; NPG., 1973, p. 8, pl. 54.
BM M&LA Sloane Collection.

215 Seal Matrix of Richard Duke of Gloucester (later Richard III) as Admiral for Dorset and Somerset, 1462.
Bronze-gilt; D 76 mm (circular, with large pierced handle on reverse).

215

The matrix is engraved with a single-masted ship, the mainsail bearing the Duke's arms (Quarterly France modern and England and a label of three points ermine); on the stern the Duke's arms occur on a standard carried by a greyhound. Legend (in 'black-letter'): s' : RICI DUC : GLOUC : ADMIRALLI : ANGL' : I : COM : DORS · &. SOMS : Richard was created Duke of Gloucester on 1 November 1461, and Lord High Admiral of England nearly a year later. The ermine label on his arms usually bore a canton gules on each point, but these were no doubt too difficult to engrave legibly on the matrix.

Bibliography: Tonnochy, 1952, no. 27; NPG., 1973, no. 145.
BM M&LA 80, 3–10, 1.

216 Shield of Arms of Henry VIII impaling Jane Seymour, *c.* 1536–40.
Stained glass; 457 × 368 mm.

The Royal arms impaling those of Seymour (six quarterings) are enclosed within a wreath of green foliage, white and red roses and a lion's mask. The first of the Seymour quarterings (Vert on a pile gules between six fleurs-de-lis azure three lions passant guardant or) is a coat of augmentation granted by the King as Jane was not of royal blood. She was married to Henry VIII, as his third wife, in 1536 and died a few days after giving birth to the future Edward VI in 1537. The shield is said to be from the destroyed palace of Nonsuch (Surrey), begun in 1538 (see also no. 68).

Bibliography: Rackham, 1936, p. 61. Lent by the Victoria and Albert Museum (Dept. of Ceramics no. C. 454–1919).

217 Seal of Jane Seymour, Third Wife of King Henry VIII, 1537.
Red wax; D 95 mm.

The Royal arms of England impaling the arms of Seymour (see no. 216) are shown on a shield surmounted by a crown and supported by the lion and unicorn.
BL Additional Charter 36198.

218 An Armorial Binding for King Henry VIII, *c.* 1540.
237 × 164 × 40 mm.

A MS description of the Holy Land, in French, by Martin Brion, dedicated to Henry VIII. Crimson velvet binding embroidered in coloured silks, gold thread and seed pearls with the initials of the King and the Royal arms surrounded by the Garter.
Bibliography: Fletcher, 1895, Pl. IX.
BL Royal MS. 20 A. iv.

219 An Armorial Binding for Queen Catherine Parr, *c.* 1545.
F. Petrarch, *Canzoniere*, Venice, 1544.
215 × 150 × 32 mm.

Purple velvet, embroidered with gold and silver thread and coloured silks with the arms of Catherine Parr, Queen consort of Henry VIII and his sixth wife.
Bibliography: Fletcher, 1895, Pl. XIV.
BL C.27.e.19.

220 A Binding with the Arms of Scotland, *c.* 1566.
The Actis and Constitutiounis of the Realme of Scotland, Edinburgh, 1566.
285 × 195 × 32 mm.

Brown calf, tooled in gold with the arms of Scotland and MARIA REGINA (Mary, Queen of Scots), in the centre; decorated with paint. Restored.
Bibliography: Fletcher, 1895, Pl. XVII.
BL C.15.b.11.

221 An Armorial Binding by Jean de Planche for Queen Elizabeth I, *c.* 1566.
N. de Nicolay, *Les quatres premiers livres des Navigations et Peregrinations Orientales*, Lyons, 1566.
353 × 240 × 35 mm.

Dark olive morocco with corner inlays of gold-blocked white leather, and tooled in gold with a large centre cartouche containing the arms and initials of Queen Elizabeth painted on an oval vellum inlay.
Bibliography: Fletcher, 1895, Pl. XVIII.
BL C.18.c.8.

222 Second Great Seal of Queen Elizabeth I, 1585–1603.
Dark green wax; D 155 mm.

The seal shows the Queen in robes of majesty between two shields of the Royal arms, each within the Garter and surmounted by a crown royal (obverse). The reverse shows the Queen on horseback, and above a rose, a harp and a fleur-de-lis, each with a crown, symbolising the kingdoms of England, Ireland and France. From the matrix designed by Nicholas Hilliard and engraved by him and Derick Anthony in 1584.
Bibliography: Birch, i, no. 490; E. Auerbach, *Nicholas Hilliard*, London, 1961, pp. 20–21, 181–86.
BL Seal no. xxxvi. 19.

218

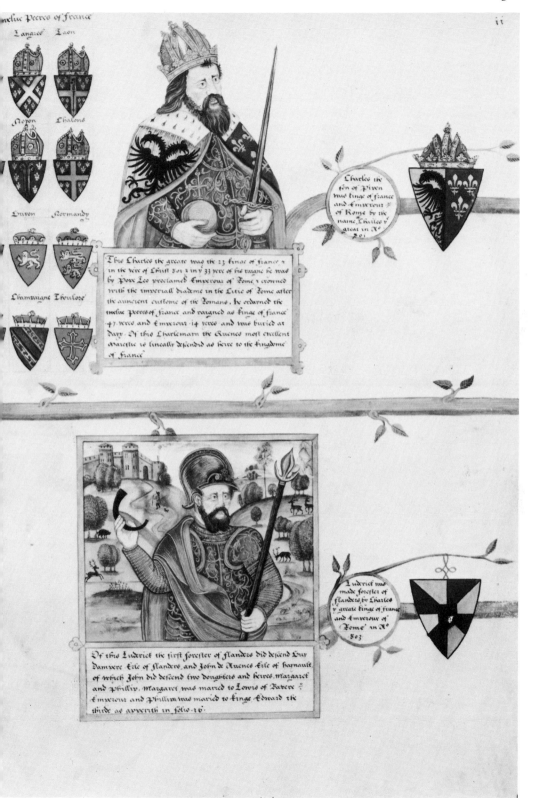

223　Illuminated Genealogy of Queen Elizabeth I, sixteenth century. Vellum; 455 × 320 mm.

The genealogy in this MS. volume is painted in the form of a tree showing the descent of Queen Elizabeth from various royal and noble European lines. The decoration includes imaginary portraits of several of the most eminent figures (on the exhibited pages, ff. 13v.–14, Charlemagne and Luderick, Forester of Flanders), and almost every person shown is given real or imaginary arms. The genealogy has been attributed to Robert Cooke, Clarenceux King of Arms 1567–93, a skilful herald painter. *Bibliography*: G. F. Warner and J. P. Gilson, *B.M. Cat. of Western MSS. in the Old Royal and King's Collections*, iii, London, 1921, pp. 65–66.
BL. Kings MS. 396.

224　Letters Patent of James I with Great Seal, 1610. Vellum; 530 × 670 mm (Seal, D 150 mm).

Letters Patent of James I, in Latin, creating his elder son Henry Prince of Wales and Earl of Chester. The miniature enclosed in the opening initial shows James bestowing the patent on Henry, the faces being the work of a skilled painter, possibly Isaac Oliver. The border decoration includes in the upper margin the Royal arms with a label of three points argent for Prince Henry, the Royal arms of the King and the Prince of Wales's badge of three ostrich feathers; on the left are the arms of the Principality of Wales (Quarterly, Or and gules, four lions passant counterchanged); on the right those of the Duchy of Cornwall (Sable fifteen bezants, 5, 4, 3, 2 and 1) and the Earldom of Chester (Azure three garbs or). *Bibliography*: Croft-Murray and Hulton, 1960, p. xvii.
BL Additional MS. 36932.

225　Great Seal of Queen Henrietta Maria, Wife of King Charles I, 1625–69. Dark green wax; D 111 mm.

Full-length portrait of the Queen between shields of arms of England and of France (obverse). The reverse shows an ornamental lozenge-shaped shield of the English Royal arms impaling those of France and Navarre impaled; the shield is surmounted by a crown royal and supported by a lion (dexter) and by an angel with a tunic semé of fleurs-de-lis (sinister). *Bibliography*: Birch, i, no. 809.
BL Seal nos. xxxiv. 16 A, B (proof impressions).

226　Seal Matrix of the Parliament of the Commonwealth, 1649–55. Bronze; D 62 mm.

Engraved with the arms of England (the cross of St George) and Ireland (a harp), placed side by side. The rim inscription reads: THE SEALE OF THE PARLIAMENT OF THE COMMON-WEALTH OF ENGLAND. The matrix was probably the work of Thomas Simon, Chief Engraver to the Mint between 1645 and 1665.
BM M&LA 1963, 4–3, 2. (Gift of Mrs E. W. Fuller in memory of her husband)

227　Dish with the Royal Arms, 1660–85. Red earthenware, covered on the upper side with white slip and decorated with dark- and light-red slip; D 564 mm.

The blazoning of the shield is incorrect, being a major simplification of the Royal arms of the Stuarts. The Royal arms, encircling Garter, the motto, the crest, mantling and supporters are accompanied by the royal cypher, 'CR' (for Charles II) and the potter's name, 'thomas TOFT'. Little is known about the Toft family, the most famous name associated with these large slipware dishes made in Staffordshire about 1670–80. *Bibliography*: R. Cooper, *English Slipware Dishes 1650–1850*, London, 1968, pp. 55–56, Pls. 145–8.
BM M&LA 1916, 5–6, 1. (Given by Lady Wernher)

228　First Great Seal of Catherine of Braganza, Wife of King Charles II, 1662. Red wax; D 120 mm.

227

226

Full-length portrait of the Queen
between shields of arms of England
and of Portugal (obverse). The
reverse shows an ornamental shield
of the English Royal arms impaling
those of Portugal, supported on the
dexter side by a lion, on the sinister
side by a wyvern.
Bibliography: Birch, i, no. 813.
BL Seal nos. xxxiv. 26 A, B (proof
impressions).

**229 Goblet and Cover with the
Royal Arms of Queen Anne,**
1707–14.
Colourless glass, faceted and
ornamented with wheel-engraved
decoration; H 301 mm.

Engraved on one side of the bowl
with the Royal arms as used by
Queen Anne from the time of the
Act of Union with Scotland (1707)
until the end of her reign in 1714;
below, the motto: SEMPER EADEM
(which Queen Anne used in
preference to 'Dieu et Mon Droit').
Engraved on the other side of the
bowl with the royal cypher, 'AR',
beneath a royal crown. Made in
Saxony and engraved in Dresden
between 1707–14, perhaps as a
special presentation gift by the
Elector of Saxony's ambassador to
the court of St James's in London.
Bibliography: British Museum
exhib. cat., *Masterpieces of Glass,*
1968, no. 246.
BM M&LA 1965, 4–5, 1.

**230 Cup and Saucer with the Arms
of William IV, Prince of Orange, and
his Wife Anne, Daughter of
George II,** 1734–35.
Porcelain, decorated in enamels;
H 36 mm (cup), D 116 mm (saucer).

The cup and saucer each bear the
conjoined arms of the Nassau
Princes of Orange, enclosed by the
Garter and motto, and the Royal
arms as used between 1714 and
1801; above is a royal crown. Both
of the shields are inaccurately
rendered in certain details. Prince
William (d. 1751) in 1733 was
elected a Knight of the Garter, and
his marriage with Princess Anne
took place in 1734.
Bibliography: Howard, 1974, p. 797.
BM OA Franks 798 +.

229

231 Double Matrix of the Judicial Seal for the Court of Great Sessions in North Wales (Division of Caernarvon, Merioneth and Anglesey), 1760–1801.
Silver; D 109 mm (circular, with three loops and three pegs).

The obverse is engraved with the equestrian figure of George III and the Prince of Wales's badge and motto; the reverse bears the Royal arms as used between 1714 and 1801. The stag and greyhound supporters distinguish the division of Caernarvon, Merioneth and Anglesey. The seal was probably designed by Christopher Seaton.
Bibliography: The matrix is unpublished, but for a study of this class of seal see H. Jenkinson, 'The Great Seal of England: Deputed or Departmental Seals', *Archaeologia*, lxxxv (1935), pp. 325–30.
BM M&LA 1976, 1–1, 1. (Gift of the Lord Chancellor)

232 Plate with Arms of the Duke of Clarence, 1789.

Porcelain, painted in colours, with gilding; on reverse, mark (in underglaze blue): 'Flight', between a crown and an open crescent; D 246 mm.

Painted with the Royal arms in use between 1714 and 1801, differenced by a label of three points (the central one with a cross of St George, the others with an anchor azure) and the insignia of the Garter and the Thistle between sprays of oak and olive; on the rim are twined ribbons of the two Orders enclosing insignia and sprays of rose and thistle. Part of a service made at Thomas Flight's factory in Worcester after Prince William Henry was created Duke of Clarence and St Andrews in 1789. In 1830 he became King as William IV. The heater-shaped shield reflects the influence of the Gothic Revival.
Bibliography: Hobson, 1905, no. V.83, Fig. 68; Hobson, 1910, p. 146, Pl. CV (3).
BM M&LA (Queen Adelaide and Franks Collection).

233 King's Messenger Badge, 1801–16.
Silver-gilt and crystal; H 131 mm.

The oval badge is surmounted by a Royal crown and bears under crystal the painted Royal arms as used between 1801 and 1816. Above the shield is G III R and flanking it are a rose and thistle all within a Garter. A silver greyhound is suspended from the bottom.
Bibliography: Montague Guest Cat., no. 1548.
BM M&LA Montague Guest No. 1548.

234 Double Matrix of the Seal for the Court of Common Pleas, 1816–17.
Silver, hall-marked London, 1816–17; D 113 mm (circular, with three loops and three pegs).

The obverse has the Royal arms as used between 1816 and 1837, supported by a wyvern and greyhound. The reverse is engraved with George III enthroned between Justice, Minerva, Hercules, Britannia and Religion. Probably

232

designed by Thomas Wyon the
Elder (d. 1830), Chief Engraver of
the Seals.
Bibliography: Tonnochy, 1952, no.
19.
BM M&LA 58, 4–13, 8. (Gift of the
Lord President of the Council)

235 Lord Chancellor's Burse for the Great Seal, 1816–20.
407 × 432 mm.

Red velvet, on the front a panel of
applied red and blue satin and
linen embroidered with silver-gilt
and silver thread, bullion, coil, strip
and purl; elaborately padded, laid
and couched work with embroidered
decoration in coloured silks, seed
pearls and spangles. Trimmed with
tassels, cord and braid of silk and
metal threads. Within a border of
cherubs' heads are the Royal arms
as used between 1816 and 1837,
enclosed by the Garter and motto
and with lion and unicorn
supporters. The crown above is
flanked by the initials GR 3, for
George III. The velvet burse
was used to contain the Great Seal
and frequently appears in portraits
of Lord Chancellors and Keepers of
the Great Seal.
Lent by the Victoria and Albert
Museum (Dept. of Textiles no.
351–1870).

236 Double Matrix of the Seal for the Court of Common Pleas (?), 1838–39.
Silver, hall-marked London, 1838–
39; D 135 mm.

The obverse is engraved with Queen
Victoria enthroned under a Gothic
canopy between personifications of
Justice and Religion; the reverse
bears the Royal arms as used since
1837, within the Garter and
supported by a lion and wyvern.
Designed by Benjamin Wyon, Chief
Engraver of the Seals.
Bibliography: Tonnochy, 1952, no.
951.
BM M&LA 1937, 6–11, 3.

235

VII

The Orders of the Garter and of the Bath

The Order of the Garter

The Order of the Garter is not only the earliest English order of chivalry, but the most ancient in Europe. Despite much research and speculation, its precise origins are still obscure. It is generally agreed that the Order was founded on St George's Day, 1348, and was connected with the establishment of a chantry college and almshouse for impoverished knights in Windsor Castle. The Order comprised the Sovereign (Edward III) and twenty-five Knights companions, including the King's son, Edward the Black Prince (no. 255). All of these Founder-Knights had taken part in the recent English campaigns in France, and the Order seems to have been conceived as a brotherhood of the King's close companions in arms. The underlying reason behind the adoption of the Garter device and motto HONY SOIT QUI MAL Y PENSE ('Evil be to him who evil thinks') remains elusive; the later story that King Edward, having been jeered by his knights for picking up a garter belonging to his mistress Joan, Countess of Salisbury, replied that they would soon hold the garter in the highest reverence and consequently chose this as the emblem of his new order, remains only a tradition.

Although the Statutes have been revised on several occasions, the Order has not been fundamentally altered since its inception. The number of Knights companions has remained at twenty-five, each with their stall-plate in St George's Chapel, Windsor Castle (nos. 258, 259), in addition to the Sovereign. In the late eighteenth and early nineteenth centuries, the Order was enlarged to include the descendants of George III and George IV; since then these (and the foreign members) have been considered extra or super-numerary to the Sovereign and twenty-five Knights. Although each Knight companion was and is elected by the Order, in practice the bestowal of the Garter has been at the direction of the Sovereign, and has been a means of honouring soldiers, personal friends and distinguished statesmen (nos. 248, 258). During the fifteenth and sixteenth centuries the election of foreign rulers to the Order was frequently employed for diplomatic ends (no. 246).

In addition to the Knights companions, the Order has its Officers. The Prelate (traditionally the Bishop of Winchester), Gentleman Usher of the Black Rod and the Register (the Dean of Windsor) have formed part of the Order from the beginning. Under Henry V the office of Garter King of Arms was introduced, the first holder of which was William Bruges (no. 237). In Edward IV's reign a Chancellor was added to the establishment (no. 244).

The Knights companions and Officers of the Order have always worn distinctive dress and regalia. The Garter knee-band is worn by the Knights on the left leg just below the knee. The earliest representation of this is on

Interior of St George's Chapel, Windsor, showing the stalls and banners of the Knights of the Garter

the effigy of Sir William Fitzwaryn (d. 1361) in Wantage church (Berks.), and the first surviving knee-band dates from *c.* 1489 (no. 246). Frequently these have been lavishly embellished with gold mounts and jewels (no. 247). The Ladies associated with the Order did not wear the Garter on the leg, but on the left arm, as shown on the effigy of Alice de la Pole, Duchess of Suffolk (d. 1475), in Ewelme church (Oxon.).

On the great ceremonies of the Order, viz., the election of a Knight and the processions and services on St George's Day (nos. 239–241), the Sovereign and Knights have worn a mantle, surcoat and hood. From at least the early fifteenth century the mantle has been embroidered with the cross of St George enclosed in a Garter on the left shoulder. Except for a brief period between 1564 and 1637 when purple was adopted (nos. 243, 249), the colour of the mantle has been blue. In Henry VII's reign a cap and an elaborate collar were introduced; under Henry VIII the precise form and materials of the collar were regulated. Since then it has consisted of twenty-six enamelled roses separated by gold knots with a jewelled pendant of St George (the 'Great George') suspended from it (no. 250). The collar could be worn on occasions other than the ceremonies associated with the Order. In the same reign the 'Lesser George', a pendant jewel worn by the Knights as part of their everyday apparel, was introduced (nos. 251–253). Under Charles I, an embroidered cross of St George within a Garter and rays was added to the insignia worn on non-ceremonial occasions (no. 254).

The Officers of the Order, the Canons of St George's and the Poor Knights also have distinctive dress. All the Officers wear mantles with the cross of St George on the shoulder, but only the Prelate and Chancellor (nos. 241, 244) encircle it by the Garter. In addition, the Chancellor, Garter King of Arms and Gentleman Usher have their own badges and insignia (nos. 245, 101, 102). The Canons wear a purple mantle with the cross of St George over a surplice (no. 241). The Poor Knights (since 1833 known as the Military Knights) for long had a blue mantle with the cross of St George on the shoulder (nos. 240, 241), but since the last century have worn scarlet tail-coats.

The Order of the Bath

Compared with the Order of the Garter, that of the Bath is a recent creation. It can lay tenuous claim, however, to an even more ancient origin. In the Middle Ages knighthood could be secured either by simply dubbing with a sword or by a much more elaborate ceremony which involved the purification of candidates by bathing. The earliest records of the latter practice can be traced back to the twelfth century; by the early fourteenth century, the bathing ceremony seems to have taken place in association with special events such as the coronation or marriage of a monarch. From at least the early fifteenth century knights so created were known as Knights of the Bath, but they were not organised into a chivalric order such as that of the Garter. It is from the same century that we have the first pictorial record of the ceremony of creating a Bath knight, perhaps that which took place on the eve of the Coronation in 1487 of Henry VII's Queen, Elizabeth of York (no. 262). By this time the Knights wore distinctive dress, to which was added in James I's reign a badge consisting of three crowns and the motto

TRIA IUNCTA IN UNO (alluding to the union of England, Scotland and Ireland under one monarch). Knights of the Bath continued to be created throughout the sixteenth and seventeenth centuries, down to the Coronation of Charles II (no. 263). From this time onwards the ancient ceremony fell into disuse.

When Knights of the Bath next appeared, in 1725, it was under a totally new guise. The prime mover behind the revival was John Anstis the Elder (nos. 98, 264), and he created a new order of chivalry, closely modelled on that of the Garter. The first investiture was held on 27 May 1725, when the Statutes drawn up by Anstis were promulgated. On 17 June the formal ceremonies, consisting of a procession, investiture and banquet, took place (no. 264); these ceremonies did not include, and never have since, the ancient rite of purification by bathing. The Order established by Anstis comprised the Sovereign, a Prince of the Blood, the Great Master and thirty-five Knights companions; the first Knight was Prince William Augustus, later Duke of Cumberland (nos. 264, 265). In common with the Garter, the Order was given several Officers, consisting in this case of Secretary, Register, Gentleman Usher, Messenger, Genealogist and Blanc Coursier Herald, and Bath King of Arms, with the Dean of Westminster acting as Dean to the Order. Again like the Garter, the Order of the Bath was given a chapel, in this case Henry VII's Chapel in Westminster Abbey, where the banners of the Knights are displayed. Except for a period between 1812 and the end of the nineteenth century, the Knights companions have also displayed their stall-plates in the Chapel.

The dress and insignia of the Knights from the inception of the Order have comprised a red mantle, which bore some relation to earlier dress worn by Knights of the Bath, a surcoat, a gold collar with the Order's badge suspended from it, a star worn on the mantle, and a small pendant badge worn, like the 'Lesser George', on non-ceremonial occasions (no. 267). The Officers of the Order also have their own distinctive badges (no. 266).

In 1815, after the conclusion of the Napoleonic Wars, the Order was expanded to include the numerous army and navy officers who had distinguished themselves in the fighting. Two new Military classes were introduced, in addition to a small number of Civil Knights. Finally, in 1847, Queen Victoria added two Civil Divisions. The Order as it has existed since then consists of three classes, each organised into Military and Civil Divisions. The First Class comprises the Knights Grand Cross, the second the Knights Commanders, and the third the Companions.

Officers of the Order of the Garter in the early sixteenth century (Writhe's Garter Book – see cat. no. 262). [*N.B. Officers shown are:— Prelate, Chancellor, Register, Garter King of Arms, Black Rod]

Select Bibliography

Anstis, J., *Observations Introductory to an Historical Essay upon the Knighthood of the Bath*, London, 1725.

Ashmole, E., *The Institution, Laws and Ceremonies of the Most Noble Order of the Garter*, London, 1672.

Beltz, G. F. *Memorials of the Most Noble Order of the Garter*, London, 1841.

Nevinson, J. C., 'The Earliest Dress and Insignia of the Knights of the Garter', *Apollo*, xlvii (1948), pp. 80–83.

——, 'The Robes of the Order of the Bath', *The Connoisseur*, cxxxiv (1954), pp. 153–59.

Risk, J. C., *The History of the Order of the Bath and its Insignia*, London, 1972.

237 William Bruges' Garter Book,
c. 1430.
Paper; 385 × 282 mm.

This armorial, the earliest known
for an order of chivalry, was
executed for William Bruges
(d. 1450), the first Garter King of
Arms. Full-page coloured drawings
show Edward III, the twenty-five
Founder-Knights of the Garter, and,
as a frontispiece, Garter King of
Arms kneeling before St George.
The figures wear blue Garter
mantles over surcoats displaying
their arms. Their right hands rest
on frames enclosing painted shields
of arms of the successors to their
stalls in St George's Chapel,
Windsor. Bruges' Garter Book has
been called the prototype of a whole
class of 'Visitations with men at
arms', another early example being

the Military Roll (no. 70). Figures
from this manuscript were
engraved by Wenceslas Hollar for
Ashmole's history of the Garter.
Bibliography: Aspilogia I, pp. 83–86,
Pl. VII; *Aspilogia* II, p. 271; Wright,
1973, pp. 9, 16–17, Pl. 10;
Stanford London, 1970.
BL Stowe MS. 594.

**238 Sir Thomas Wriothesley's
Garter Book,** *c.* 1524.
Vellum; 300 × 353 mm.

A volume of the Statutes of the
Orders of the Garter, of the Golden
Fleece, and of St Michael of France,
with other miscellaneous heraldic
material, written and illuminated for
Sir Thomas Wriothesley, Garter
(1505–34). The Statutes of the
Garter are preceded by a painting of
the arms of the Sovereign within a
Garter collar (for a similar painting

of the collar see no. 72). A border
is formed of shields of arms of the
Knights companions of the Order as
between 23 April 1524 (election of
Arthur Plantagenet, Viscount Lisle,
and Robert Radcliffe, 9th Lord
Fitzwalter) and 21 May 1524
(death of Thomas Howard, 2nd
Duke of Norfolk). On the right hand
exhibited page the initial letter of the
Statutes encloses the Royal arms,
and in the lower margin occur the
arms of Wriothesley between the
initials 'Th. Wr' and his crest of a
bull's head. Further decoration in
this manuscript includes two
coloured drawings of the House of
Lords in the times of Edward I and
Henry VIII (ff. 8, 60).
Bibliography: SAHE., no. 171;
BHA., p. 66.
Lent by Her Majesty The Queen
(Windsor Heraldic MS. 2).

237

238

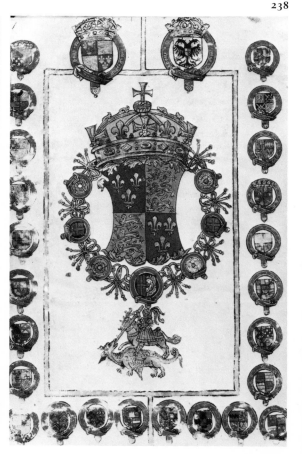

240

239 King Henry VIII and his Garter Knights in the Register or Black Book of the Order of the Garter, *c.* 1534.
Vellum; 420 × 300 mm.

This register is known from its binding as the 'Black Book' of the Order of the Garter and is the second register of the Order (the first, begun in the reign of Henry V, is lost). The Black Book contains the Statutes in Latin, an account of the foundation of the Order, and the ceremonies and installations of the reigns of Henry VIII and Edward VI. The first part of the book was written about 1534. The exhibited painting occurs at the beginning of the acts of Henry VIII's reign and covers two full pages (pp. 194–5).
At the top left Henry VIII sits enthroned, surrounded by twenty-five Knights in mantles and collars of the Order. Below, the Knights, wearing armorial surcoats over their mantles, appear in a procession which advances across both pages. At the top right the three leading Knights in the procession have arrived in St George's Chapel and move forward to the altar. The text

places this occasion in the twenty-sixth year of Henry's reign (1534). This suggests that the miniature depicts only a formal view of a procession of the Knights, for King Henry was absent from the chapter of 1534 and Garter King of Arms (Sir Thomas Wriothesley, d. 1534) was excused from attending 'being worn out with Age and reduced by a grievous Decay.' On the right of Garter as shown in the picture is the scribe or Register of the Order in a white surplice. This is possibly Robert Aldridge, a Canon of Windsor (afterwards Provost of Eton), who was appointed scribe on 27 May 1534 and was then responsible for keeping the Black Book. Following Garter in the procession come the Kings of Spain, Scotland and France, the Emperor Charles V, and Henry VIII behind his sword-bearer.
Bibliography: J. Anstis, *The Register of the Most Noble Order of the Garter . . . called the Black Book*, London, ii, 1724, pp. 268 and 4 plates following, 393, Appendix xii; E. Auerbach, 'The Black Book of the Garter', *Report of the Soc. of the Friends of St George's*, v, no. 4

(1972–3), pp. 149–53, Pls. 1–9; Windsor, 1975, no. 77.
Lent by the Most Noble Order of the Garter through the Dean of Windsor as Register. Windsor Aerary (G1).

240 Procession of the Knights of the Garter by Marcus Gheeraerts the Elder, 1576.
Coloured etching; 378 × 544 mm (each sheet).

A set of nine sheets originally forming a roll, depicting the procession of the Knights on St George's Day, 1576. The procession moves from left to right and is led (sheet 1) by the Verger. Then follow (2) the Poor Knights, (3 and 4) the heralds and pursuivants, including Robert Cooke and Robert Glover, (5, 6, 7) the Knights companions with their arms, of whom the last (8) is the Emperor Maximilian II; he precedes (8) Gentleman-Usher of the Black Rod, the Register of the Order and Garter King of Arms (Gilbert Dethick); behind this group are the Chancellor and Prelate of the Order, two Gentlemen-Ushers, (9) the Queen's sword-bearer, and finally

Queen Elizabeth I. The figures are set in front of an arcade with Renaissance architectural details, through which is a view of Windsor Castle. In the cartouches are identifications in French. These were almost certainly provided by Thomas Dawes, Rouge-Croix Pursuivant (1570–c. 1580) who also signed the dedication to the Queen. In 1786 Sir John Fenn, who owned the roll at the time, added the English labels at the bottom. The general design has been attributed to Dawes. The engraver, Marcus Gheeraerts the Elder, was a Flemish artist who fled to England as a Protestant refugee in 1568. There are two other known impressions of the Procession, neither of them coloured.
Bibliography: A. M. Hind, *Engraving in England in the Sixteenth and Seventeenth Centuries,* i, Cambridge, 1952, pp. 104–21; R. Strong, 'Queen Elizabeth I and the Order of the Garter', *Arch. J.,* cxix (1962), pp. 249–51, Pls. XXXVIII–XXXIX.
BM P&D 1892–6–28–194.

241 Drawings from Sir Peter Lely's Garter Ceremonies, 1663–71. Black oiled chalk, heightened with white, on blue-grey paper; 510 × 375 mm.

1) The Prelate of the Order, George Morley, Bishop of Winchester, walking towards the left and looking over his shoulder. He wears a skull-cap and mantle with the cross of St George within the Garter on the shoulder, and in his right hand he holds an academic cap.
2) Two Canons of Windsor engaged in conversation. They each wear a skull-cap and mantle with the cross of St George over a surplice and cassock; the right figure holds an academic cap in his left hand, his companion a book.
3) Two Poor Knights of Windsor, walking towards the left and conversing. They wear mantles with the cross of St George; the left figure holds a walking-stick.
4) A Knight companion wearing the mantle and collar of the Order and with a plumed hat on his head.

These four drawings are part of a large series executed by Sir Peter Lely between 1663 and 1671 (see no. 92).
Bibliography: See no. 92.
BM P&D (1) 1862–7–12–647; (2) 1862–7–12–652; (3) 1862–7–12–646; (4) 1847–5–29–12.

242 Miniature of the Earl of Shrewsbury in Garter Robe, c. 1445. Vellum; 465 × 320 mm.

This manuscript of poems and romances in French was presented to Margaret of Anjou by John Talbot, 1st Earl of Shrewsbury, K. G., probably on the occasion of her marriage to King Henry VI in 1445, when the Earl was employed to escort her to England. In the exhibited miniature (f. 2v), the work of a French artist, the Earl is shown accompanied by a Talbot dog and kneeling to offer his manuscript to the Queen. He wears a red robe semé with Garters and carries a hood on his left shoulder. Robes of this kind were ordinary Court wear for Garter Knights and were given as regular yearly gifts from the King. At the end of the volume (f. 439) there is a miniature of the Sovereign and Knights in a chapter of the Order kneeling before St George; there they are wearing their ceremonial mantles decorated with Garters. A copy of the early Statutes accompanies this picture. On the facing exhibited page (f. 3) is a richly illuminated genealogical table in the form of a fleur-de-lis showing French and English royal descents from St Louis, uniting in the figure of King Henry VI of England. This fleur-de-lis genealogy has been identified as a copy of a picture made in about 1423 as propaganda for King Henry VI's claim to France. The original was executed for Henry's uncle the Duke of Bedford, Regent of France, who had it hung with an accompanying poem in Notre Dame. Copies were made of the picture and the explanatory verses (later translated into English by John Lydgate) and they were probably circulated; it is presumably from

one of these that Talbot derived his version, the only example of the picture now remaining.
Bibliography: British Museum, *Reproductions from Illuminated Manuscripts,* Series II, 1923, Pl. XXIX; B. J. H. Rowe, 'King Henry VI's Claim to France in Picture and Poem', *The Library,* xi (1932–33), pp. 77–88; W. A. Rees-Jones, *Saint George, The Order of St. George and the Church of St. George in Stamford,* London, 1937, Pl. VII; J. W. McKenna, 'Henry VI of England and the Dual Monarchy: Aspects of Royal Political Propaganda, 1422–1432', *J. Warburg and Courtauld Insts.,* xxviii (1965), pp. 145–62.
BL Royal MS. 15 E. vi.

243 Miniature of a Knight of the Garter in an 'Album Amicorum', c. 1616–18. Paper; 96 × 163 mm.

The Knight of the Garter (f. 24) is shown with garter, collar and mantle of the Order, the mantle being purple in colour at this date (between 1564 and 1637). This album was kept by Frederic of Botnia. In addition to autographs collected by the owner at Saumur from 1616 to 1618, it contains a series of paintings which include English royal personages and other dignitaries. This series of miniatures, with among them the Garter Knight, appears in several albums of the early seventeenth century, and was probably collected as a 'souvenir' of a visit to England.
Bibliography: Nickson, 1970, pp. 18–19.
BL Additional MS. 16889.

244 Plaque depicting Bishop Burnet, Chancellor of the Order of the Garter, early eighteenth century. Ivory; H 93 mm.

The half-length figure of Burnet is shown wearing the Order's mantle with the cross of St George on the right shoulder. Gilbert Burnet (1643–1715), Bishop of Salisbury, was an extremely tolerant man by the standards of his time. A firm

243 △

△245

246 △   ▽244

opponent of James II, he played a large part in his replacement on the throne by William and Mary.
Bibliography: Dalton, 1909, no. 426, Pl. CIII.
BM M&LA Sloane Collection No. 360.

245 Pendant Badge of the Chancellor of the Order of the Garter, seventeenth century(?).
D 38 mm.

On the obverse is a rose within the Garter and motto, in enamel on a gold base; the reverse bears a cross of St George within the Garter and motto. The suspension loop is gold. This badge was first assigned to the Chancellor of the Order in the reign of Philip and Mary.
BM M&LA 1909, 6–5, 2. (Given through the National Art Collections Fund)

246 Garter of Maximilian I, King of the Romans, c. 1489.
L 540 mm.

The silk Garter has a gold and enamelled buckle and Tudor roses between the words of the motto, which are embroidered in gold thread. On the reverse an engraved plate bears a very worn shield of arms which have been identified as those of Maximilian, King of the Romans. He was elected a Knight of the Garter in 1489. In 1493 he became Holy Roman Emperor and died in 1519. This is the earliest surviving Garter.
Bibliography: C. R. Beard, 'The Emperor Maximilian's Garter', *The Connoisseur*, cxxxi (1953), pp. 108–109; Windsor, 1975, no. 106. Lent by the National Trust, Anglesey Abbey (Cambs.).

247 Garter of Frederick II, King of Denmark, 1581.
L 550 mm.

Blue velvet with edging of pearls. The buckle-mounts are in enamelled gold set with tablecut diamonds and rubies. The words of the motto are also set with rubies in gold mounts. This Garter belonged to King Frederick II of Denmark, who having been elected to the Order in 1578, was invested as a Knight companion in 1581. The lavish embellishment of this Garter corresponds closely with the descriptions of Garters sent from England in the sixteenth and seventeenth centuries to various European sovereigns on their becoming Knights.
Bibliography: Christensen, 1940, p. 30, Pl. IV; Nevinson, 1948, p. 81.
Lent by the Danish Royal Collections, Rosenborg Castle.

248 Garter of Lord Palmerston, 1856.
Blue velvet with gold motto and buckle; L 371 mm.

This Garter was worn by the statesman Henry John Temple, Viscount Palmerston (1784–1865), created K.G. in 1856.
BM M&LA 1944, 10–1, 16. (Gift of Miss M. Turner).

249 Garter Mantle of Christian IV, King of Denmark and Norway, 1606.
Velvet, lined with white taffeta; L 3·560 m.

The mantle is purple and has a shield bearing the cross of St George within a Garter embroidered on the left shoulder. For most of the Order's history the mantle has been blue, but between 1564 and 1637 it was purple. Christian IV was James I of England's brother-in-law and was installed as a Knight by proxy in 1605. Presumably this was the mantle sent by James to him in 1606. In the warrant it is described as '. . . one Robe of Purple Velvet of our Noble Order of the Garter . . . and also one Garter to set upon the shoulder of the same Robe, richly embroidered upon Blue Velvet, with sundry sorts of Pearls, Purls, Plates, Venice Twists and Silk . . .' This is the earliest surviving Garter mantle.
Bibliography: Ashmole, 1672, Appendix LXXIX; Christensen, 1940, pp. 21–28, Pls. I and II; Nevinson, 1948, p. 83.
Lent by the Danish Royal Collections, Rosenborg Castle.

250 Collar and Great George of the 1st Earl of Northampton, 1628–29.
L 1·550 m (collar), H 70 mm (Great George).

The collar consists of twenty-five (there should be twenty-six) enamelled gold roses within Garters (corresponding with the number of Knights companions of the Order) linked by twenty-five gold knots (one is missing). Suspended from the collar is the Great George, comprising the mounted figure of St George slaying the dragon, in enamelled gold and set with diamonds. The collar was made for William Compton, 1st Earl of Northampton, who was elected a Knight of the Garter in 1628, was installed in 1629 and died in 1630. This is one of the three oldest surviving Garter collars.
The wearing of distinctive collars by the Knights of the Garter began in Henry VII's reign and their design and material were regulated under Henry VIII (see the Introduction to this section).
Lent by the Earl Compton.

Colour plate.

251 Pendant Lesser George, seventeenth century.
68 × 50 mm.

The obverse has a gold-mounted onyx cameo of St George slaying the dragon within the Garter and motto, enclosed in a border of cabochon jewels. On the reverse is an embossed silver-gilt relief of St George and the dragon within an enamelled Garter and motto. The Lesser George was introduced during Henry VIII's reign to be worn by Knights of the Order on non-ceremonial occasions.
BM M&LA 1920, 11–17, 1.
Colour plate.

249

252 Pendant Lesser George,
seventeenth century.
43 × 32 mm.

On the obverse is the equestrian
figure of St George slaying the
dragon, in coloured enamel on a
gold base; the reverse has a floral
pattern in enamel. The frame is
composed of semi-precious stones.
BM M&LA OA 2371.

253 Pendant Lesser George,
seventeenth century.
H 39 mm.

The equestrian figure of St George
slaying the dragon in coloured
enamel is set on a gold base within
a white enamel border bearing the
Order's motto in black.
BM M&LA Franks Bequest No. 2881.

**254 Medal Commemorating an
Alteration of a Garter Badge,** 1629.
Silver; D 28 mm.

On the obverse is a bust of Charles I
and the legend CAROLVS · I · D · G ·
ANG · SCOT · FRAN · ET · HIB · REX ·
FIDEI · DEF. The reverse shows the
Order's star with the legend
PRISCI · DECVS · ORDINIS · ACTVM ·
1629. In this year the Order's badge
as worn on cloaks and coats of the
Knights on ordinary occasions was
converted into a star by the addition
of a glory. The medal was executed
by Nicholas Briot (appointed Chief
Engraver to the mint in 1633).
Bibliography: Ashmole, 1672, p.
216; *Medallic Ill.*, i, no. 33, p. 253.
BM C&M M7096. (Gift of Miss Banks).

**255 Badge showing the Black
Prince within the Garter,**
late fourteenth century.
Lead; H 120 mm.

This badge shows the Black Prince,
(d. 1376), son of Edward III and a
founder member of the Order of
the Garter, kneeling before the
Trinity. An angel above holds his
shield (Quarterly France ancient and
England with a label of three
points). An angel behind him holds
his helmet with a lion crest. The
scene is encircled within the Garter
which bears the motto HONY SOYT
KE MAL Y PENSE. The tabard, shield,

255

257

helm and gauntlets worn by the
Prince are very similar to the
funeral achievements which hung
above his tomb in Canterbury
Cathedral (and are now displayed
close by); the painting on the tester
of the tomb also indicates the
devotion of the Prince to the
Trinity. The Prince kneeling before
the Trinity is also depicted on the
frontispiece of the metrical chronicle
of Sir John Chandos and in the
illumination of the initial letter of
the charter granting Aquitaine to
the Black Prince in 1362. The back
of the badge is flat and there is no
sign of any attachment. The exact
purpose of the badge is obscure,
although since the lead badge was
made in a mould this suggests that
a number of examples were produced, possibly for distribution.
Bibliography: N. H. Nicolas,
'Observations on the Institution of
the Order of the Garter', *Archaeologia*,
xxxi (1846), pp. 140–41; W. H. St
John Hope, *Heraldry for Craftsmen
and Designers*, London, 1913,
pp. 260–63, Fig. 153.
BM M&LA OA 100.

**256 Medal depicting Federigo da
Montefeltro, Duke of Urbino**
(d. 1484).
Bronze; D 114 mm.

The obverse shows the Duke's head
in profile, enclosed by the Garter
and motto. On the reverse is a
group of five putti supporting a

shield. Undoubtedly by an Italian
artist, this medallion has been
attributed to the Florentine sculptor
Pietro Torrigiano (1472–1528),
working in England between 1511
and c. 1522. However, it is more
likely to have been executed by a
late fifteenth century artist at Urbino.
Federigo, elected a Knight of the
Garter in 1474, was one of the
great patrons of Renaissance art,
employing, amongst others, Piero
della Francesca and Joos van
Ghent. In 1506 Federigo's son
Guidobaldo (elected K.G. in 1504)
sent a Raphael painting of St George
wearing the Garter knee-band to
Henry VII.
Bibliography: *Medallic Ill.*, i, no. 1,
p. 16; G. Habich, *Die Medaillen der
italienischen Renaissance*, Stuttgart
and Berlin, 1924, Pl. xxxii, no. 1;
G. F. Hill, *A Corpus of Italian Medals
of the Renaissance before Cellini*,
London, 1930, no. 1118.
BM C&M 1881–7–4–4.

**257 Shield of Arms of Thomas
Howard, 3rd Duke of Norfolk
(1473–1554), within the Garter,**
early sixteenth century (after 1524).
Stained glass; 483 × 330 mm.

The arms are Quarterly; 1, England
with a label of three points argent;
2, Gules on a bend argent between
six cross crosslets fitchy argent an
escutcheon of Scotland; 3, Checky
or and azure; 4, Gules a lion
rampant argent. The shield is set on

a green ground and the enclosing Garter bears the Order's motto; the yellow crown above is not part of the original panel which comes from Barham Hall (Suffolk). The arms of Scotland on the bend were granted by Henry VIII in 1514, in recognition of the second Duke's victory over the Scots at Flodden. Thomas became 3rd Duke in 1524. The Dukes of Norfolk are hereditary Earl Marshals of England.
Lent by the Victoria and Albert Museum (Dept. of Ceramics nos. C.798–1920 and C.400–1915).

258 Garter Stall-plate of Sir Anthony Browne, 1540.
Copper-gilt and enamelled; 167 × 123 mm.

The plate has a shield with the arms of Sir Anthony Browne (Sable on a bend cotised three lions passant or) with fourteen other quarterings, enclosed within a Garter with the Order's motto. The supporters are two wolves azure, ducally chained and gorged, with a stag statant gules as crest. At the top is a scroll bearing the motto SVYNE RAYSON, and the base has an inscription referring to Sir Anthony Browne's installation as a Knight of the Garter in 1540. The plate was

259

intended to be placed amongst those of other Knights on the stalls in St George's Chapel, Windsor Castle, but there is a stall-plate for Sir Anthony Browne at Windsor, very similar to the British Museum's plate and evidently of the same date. This is of higher quality and there are differences in the quarterings and inscriptions. Furthermore, there is at least one error in the tinctures on the Museum's plate. The evidence thus suggests that the Museum's stall-plate was a rejected piece. Sir Anthony Browne (d. 1548) was a member of the Privy Council and an intimate friend of Henry VIII. He did extremely well out of the dissolution of the monasteries and is buried in a splendid Renaissance tomb in Battle church (Sussex).
BM M&LA OA 85.

259 Garter Stall-plate of Sir William Parr, 1552.
Copper-gilt and enamelled; 256 × 165 mm.

The plate bears the arms of Parr (two bars azure within a bordure engrailed) with nine other quarterings, enclosed within the Garter and motto, and supported by a stag or and a wyvern azure; the crest is a maiden vested azure, couped below the shoulders. At the top of the plate is the motto AMOVR · AVECQVE · LOIAVLTE · and the words FVST · ENSTALLE · 18 · IVRE · DE · MAY · LANDU · REING · NRE · SOVVERAIN · SEIGNEVR · LE · ROY · HENRY · 8 · 36. Below the arms is a text giving Parr's titles and the date 1552. The plate is broken across the middle. Sir William Parr, Marquis of Northampton (1513–71), was the brother of Catherine Parr, Henry VIII's sixth wife. He became a Knight of the Garter in 1552, but in the following year was attainted for his support of Lady Jane Grey. His subsequent degradation from the Order was no doubt the occasion when the plate was removed from his stall in St George's Chapel and broken. On Queen Elizabeth's accession in 1559 Parr was re-elected to the Order, and a new stall-plate set up, which still exists.

Bibliography: A. W. Franks, 'Notice of a Stall-plate of Sir William Parr, K.G., Marquis of Northampton', *Archaeologia*, xxxvi (1855), pp. 214–18.
BM M&LA 55, 1–30, 1. (Gift of A. W. Franks).

260 Medal Commemorating the Investiture of John George IV, Elector of Saxony, as Knight of the Garter, 1693.
Silver; D 44·5 mm.

The obverse depicts a bust of the Elector with the legend IOH · GEORGE · IV · D · G · DVX · SAX · I · C · M · A · & · W · ELECT, and o.f. [ecit] for the designer, Martin Heinrich Omeis (1650–1703). On the reverse are the arms of Saxony and the Electoral cap within the Garter; legend: IVNGIMVR HOC SIGNO : QVO NON DISIVNGIMVR VNQVAM : SIC NOSTRA AETERNVM PECTORA IVNCTA MANENT. John George was elected a Knight on 2 February 1692, and invested at Dresden on 26 January 1693.
Bibliography: Medallic Ill., ii, no. 292, pp. 79–80.
BM C&M M7859. (Gift of the Earl of Enniskillen)

261 Medal Commemorating the Investiture of William V, Prince of Orange, as Knight of the Garter, 1752.
Silver; D 39 mm.

The obverse shows Prince William wearing the Garter collar; legend: WILH · V · D · G · PR · AR · ET · N · FOED · BELG · LIB · GVB · HAER and the initials I · G · H · F[ecit] ·, for the designer, Johann Georg Holtzhey (1729–1808). On the reverse is St George and the dragon within a Garter; legend: EQVES CREATVS DIE V IVNY · MDCCLII. William V, grandson of King George II of England, was elected a Knight on 13 March 1752, and was invested at the Hague on 5 June.
Bibliography: Medallic Ill., ii, no. 379, p. 669.
BM C&M M8227.

262 Paintings of the Ceremony of Knighthood of the Bath, c. 1488.
Paper; 365 × 260 mm (p. 127), 390 × 270 (p. 128).

The pages exhibited show the final scenes in a series of twenty-four illustrations of ceremonies for creating a Knight of the Bath (twenty-three paintings and one drawing – see no. 47). To conclude the rituals, which lasted two or even three days, the new Knight was dressed in a robe of blue, with a lace of white silk on the left shoulder which he must wear until he had performed a deed of prowess. His ceremonial array he gave to the heralds as their fee. In the exhibited scenes the esquire-governors take their leave of the new Knight (p. 127), and finally a noble lady removes the stigma of the white lace, witnessed by the King and the heralds, perhaps at a tournament (p. 128).

The Bath pictures appear in a composite volume known from its second item as *Writhe's Garter Book*. The volume contains miscellaneous heraldic and genealogical material, much of it compiled by John Writhe, third Garter King of Arms 1478–1504, and his son and successor, Sir Thomas Wriothesley, Garter 1505–34. Other items, some of them as late as the eighteenth century, have been added, the volume being bound up in its present form in 1827. The Bath pictures occur in an uninterrupted and indivisible sequence with surrounding Writhe material which can be dated to the late 1480s. It seems almost certain therefore that they were made for John Writhe, perhaps in connection with the creation of Knights of the Bath in 1487 on the eve of the Coronation of Elizabeth of York, Queen of Henry VII.

Other material in Writhe's Garter Book includes leaves from the late fifteenth century Salisbury Roll copy (no. 34), and also the original vellum Salisbury Roll of *c.* 1463. The latter forms one of the later additions, not being present when the volume was described in 1738 by the antiquary William Oldys, Norroy King of Arms.

Bibliography: *Aspilogia* I, pp. 122–24; *Aspilogia* II, pp. 279–80; Reading, 1963, nos. 7 and 12; Wagner, 1967, p. 138, Pls. X–XII; Stanford London, 1970, pp. 112–13; NPG., 1973, no. 133; Scott, 1976, pp. 47–54 (but see review by J. Backhouse, *Medium Aevum*, xlvii, no. 1).

Lent by His Grace the Duke of Buccleuch and Queensberry.

Colour plate

263 Painted Arms of Knights of the Bath, early seventeenth century. Vellum; 420 × 285 mm.

This book of painted arms contains shields of arms with helms, crests and mantling of Knights of the Bath from 1603 to 1625 with additions made in 1661. The exhibited pages (ff. 47v.–48) show the arms of Knights created on the eve of King James I's Coronation in 1603. An earlier section of the manuscript has sixteenth century paintings of the arms of Knights Bachelor and Knights of the Garter.

Bibliography: HCEC., no. 102, Pl. XXXV.

Lent by the College of Arms (MS. M 7).

264 The Procession and Ceremonies of the Installation of the Knights of the Bath on the Institution of the Order, 17 June 1725.
Water-colour; (1) 440 × 620 mm; (2) 210 × 625 mm; (3) 240 × 605 mm; (4) 440 × 620 mm.

Four drawings from a series made by Joseph Highmore which were subsequently engraved by John Pine (later Bluemantle Pursuivant) for his book.

(1) The installation of the Knights in Henry VII's Chapel, Westminster Abbey; The first Knight, Prince William, later Duke of Cumberland (see no. 265), is shown offering his sword to the Dean, with the other Knights standing underneath their banners.

264

265

(2) Four pursuivants, six heralds and the provincial Kings of Arms in procession.

(3) The procession of the Officers of the Order of the Bath, comprising Secretary, Register, Gentleman Usher, the Genealogist (John Anstis the Younger), in addition to Garter King of Arms (John Anstis the Elder), and Bath King of Arms. Then follows the Dean of Westminster and the Great Master (the Duke of Montagu). Finally there is the figure of Prince William.

(4) The Knights of the Order at the Great Banquet, held in the Court of Requests in Westminster Palace. Bath King of Arms is proclaiming the style of Prince William, at the bringing in of the second course.
Bibliography: Pine, 1730; Birmingham, 1936, no. 544; Wagner, 1967, pp. 350–56; Pls. XXXII, XXXIV; Cambridge, Fitzwilliam Museum, *Cat. of an Exhib. of Heraldry*, 1970, no. 42.
Cambridge, Fitzwilliam Museum, Anglesey Abbey Loan AA. 163 (MS.).
Lent by the National Trust, Anglesey Abbey (Cambs.).

265 Medal Commemorating the Founding of the Order of the Bath, 1725.
Silver; D 46 mm.

The reverse shows Prince William Augustus, later Duke of Cumberland, in the robes of a Knight of the Bath, with the legend SPES · ALTERA. At the bottom is the inscription ORD · EQVIT · DE · BALN · REST · ET · INSIG · AVCT · MDCCXXV. The obverse has a bust of George I. The medal was executed by John Croker (1670–1741). Prince William was the first Knight of the Order of the Bath as instituted by John Anstis the Elder.
Bibliography: Medallic Ill., ii, no. 75, p. 463.
BM C&M 1897–6–4–6. (Gift of Miss Banks)

266 Pendant Badge of John Anstis the Younger as Blanc Coursier Herald and Genealogist of the Order of the Bath, 1725.
H 76 mm.

The oval badge has on one side the three linked crowns device of the Order on a brown enamel ground; on the other side is a galloping white horse on a brown enamel ground and the motto: NEC ASPERA TORRENT. On the gold frame is the Bath motto: IN UNO TRIA JUNCTA. The badge is surmounted by a gold crown and suspension loop. It belonged to John Anstis the Younger (d. 1754) who was the first Genealogist of the Order (see no. 264).
Bibliography: The badge is depicted in Pine, 1730.
Lent by the Victoria and Albert Museum (Dept. of Metalwork no. M. 7–1937).

267 Pendant Badge of the Order of the Bath, eighteenth century.
Gold; H 43 mm.

The badge has the Order's device of the three crowns linked by a stem with a rose and thistle springing from it, all enclosed within a frame bearing the Order's motto.
BM M&LA Franks Bequest No. 2966.

268 Genealogy of the Sovereigns of the Order of the Bath, 1803.
Vellum; 410 × 293 mm.

This genealogy of King George III and other sovereigns of the Order of the Bath (known to heralds as 'The Bath Book') was compiled by George Nayler, Genealogist and Blanc Coursier Herald of the Order (afterwards Garter King of Arms 1822–31). A full-page portrait of George III is painted as a frontispiece and the whole is most sumptuously illuminated with arms and devices in gold and colours. The manuscript is said to have been prepared for King George III, but retained by Nayler because of the King's refusal to pay for it. At the bottom right of the exhibited pages (pp. 64–5) are the entry and arms for George III's second son, Frederick Duke of York, who was then Great Master of the Order of the Bath, and a friend and patron of Nayler.
Bibliography: HCEC., no. 133; CA., p. 64; Wagner, 1967, p. 435.
Lent by the College of Arms.

266

Glossary

Achievement A complete display of armorial bearings, i.e. shield, crest, wreath, mantling and helm, with supporters.

Annulet A ring.

Argent Silver.

Azure Blue.

Badge A device not borne on the shield, usually employed as a mark of identification, ownership or allegiance.

Banner A rectangular flag, in medieval times mounted lengthways along the lance or staff, bearing the arms of the owner; it later became a square.

Bar A horizontal band narrower than the Fess.

Barry Having a number of bars.

Base Lower part of the shield.

Bend A band running diagonally across a shield.

Bezant A gold roundel.

Billet An oblong charge.

Blazon Description of arms in heraldic language.

Bordure A narrow border around the edge of a shield.

Canting arms Arms which allude in a punning way to the bearer's name.

Canton Rectangular corner of the shield in dexter chief.

Charge Anything depicted on a shield of arms.

Checky Divided into squares like a chess board.

Chevron A figure like two rafters meeting.

Chief Upper part of the shield cut off by a horizontal line.

Couchant Descriptive of animals lying.

Counter-charged When the field is party of two different colours and a charge over the whole field has the colours reversed.

Crest A device fixed upon the helm.

Cross Fitchy A cross with a pointed lower arm.

Cross Formy A cross with splayed, straight-ended arms.

Cross Moline A cross, each arm of which terminates in a millrind.

Cross Patonce A cross with splayed arms ending in three points.

Dexter The wearer's right side of a shield, i.e. to the observer's left.

Difference Marks introduced to a coat of arms to distinguish different members of a family.

Engrailed A divisional line in the form of semicircular indents.

Erased The ragged base of an animals head or limb.

Ermine A conventional representation of the fur.

Escutcheon of pretence A small shield in the centre of the husband's shield to indicate that his wife is an heraldic heiress.

Fess A broad horizontal band across the middle of the shield.

Fetterlock A shackle.

Field Background of a shield on which the charges are placed.

Fusil A lozenge with the top and bottom elongated.

Gorged Wearing a collar around the neck.

Guardant Of a beast with its head turned towards the observer.

Gules Red.

Impaled A method of setting two coats of arms side by side on a shield, e.g. for displaying the arms of man and wife.

Label A narrow band across the top of the shield with a number of tags; used as a difference or a mark of cadency for the eldest son.

Lodged Of a beast of the chase couchant.

Lozenge A diamond-shaped figure.

Mantling Decorative drapery handing behind the helm.

Martlet A bird.

Maunch A type of medieval lady's sleeve.

Mullet Figure like a spur rowel or star with five points.

Or Gold.

Ordinary A roll of arms classified by charges, e.g. lions, griffins, etc.

Pale A vertical band down the middle of a shield.

Passant Descriptive of animals walking.

Pennon A narrow pointed lance-flag charged with the arms or armorial device of the bearer.

Powdered Scattered with small charges.

Proper In natural colours.

Purpure Purple.

Quartering Dividing a shield into quarters with a coat of arms in each. Later used less strictly for 'quarterings' of six, eight, etc.

Rampant Descriptive of a beast when in an erect position.

Reguardant Of a beast looking backwards over its shoulder.

Sable Black.

Saltire A diagonal cross or cross of St Andrew.

Sinister The bearer's left side of a shield, i.e. the observer's right.

Standard An elongated flag containing the cross of St George, and the bearer's badge and motto, but never the arms.

Supporters The human, natural or fabulous creatures on either side of a shield of arms.

Tabard A short loose outer garment worn over armour or by heralds.

Tinctures The metals, colours and furs of heraldry.

Torse A twisted wreath or band masking the join of the crest with the helm.

Trick A sketch of a shield of arms with tinctures indicated by letters.

Vair One of the furs of heraldry, represented by a conventional variegated pattern of blue and white.

Vert Green.

Canton   *Chevron*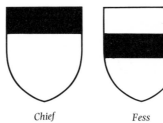
Chief   *Fess*
Pale   *Saltire*

List of Works referred to in Abbreviated form

Alexander, 1972 – J. J. G. Alexander, 'William Abell "lymnour" and 15th Century English Illumination', *Kunsthistorische Forschungen Otto Pächt zu seinem 70 Geburtstag*, Salzburg, 1972, pp. 166–72.

Amsterdam, 1973 – Amsterdam, Rijksmuseum, exhibition catalogue (by M. Archer), *English Delftware*, 1973.

Anglo, 1968 – S. Anglo, *The Great Tournament Roll of Westminster*, Oxford, 1968.

Ashmole, 1672 – E. Ashmole, *The Institution, Laws and Ceremonies of the Most Noble Order of the Garter*, London, 1672.

Aspilogia I – A. R. Wagner, *A Catalogue of English Mediaeval Rolls of Arms*, Society of Antiquaries, London, 1950.

Aspilogia II – T. D. Tremlett, H. S. London, A. R. Wagner, *Rolls of Arms Henry III (with additions and corrections to Aspilogia I)* Society of Antiquaries, London, 1967.

BHA. – London, Burlington Fine Arts Club exhibition catalogue, *British Heraldic Art to the End of the Tudor Period*, London, 1916.

Baddeley, 1908 – W. St Clair Baddeley, *A Cotswold Shrine*, London, 1908.

Barrett, 1966 – F. A. Barrett, *Worcester Porcelain and Lund's Bristol*, 2nd ed., London, 1966.

Birch – W. de G. Birch, *Catalogue of Seals in the Department of Manuscripts in the British Museum*, 6 vols., London, 1887–1900.

Birmingham, 1936 – Birmingham City Museum and Art Gallery, *Catalogue of an Heraldic Exhibition*, 1936.

Blunt, 1941–3 – C. E. Blunt, 'The Heavy Coinage of Henry IV', *British Numismatic Journal*, xxiv (1941–3), pp. 22–27.

Book Plates Cat. – E. R. J. Gambier Howe, *Franks Bequest. Catalogue of British and American Book Plates*, 3 vols., London (British Museum), 1903–4.

Brault, 1972 – G. J. Brault, *Early Blazon. Heraldic Terminology in the Twelfth and Thirteenth Centuries with Special Reference to Arthurian Literature*, Oxford, 1972.

Brault, 1973 – G. J. Brault, *Eight Thirteenth Century Rolls of Arms in French and Anglo-Norman Blazon*, Pennsylvania State University Press, 1973.

Bristol, 1970 – Bristol City Art Gallery exhibition catalogue, *Bristol Porcelain Bicentenary Exhibition*, 1970.

British Portraits Cat. – *Catalogue of Engraved British Portraits preserved in the Department of Prints and Drawings in the British Museum*, 6 vols., (vols. i–iv by F. O'Donoghue, vol. v by F. O'Donoghue, and H. M. Hake, vol. vi by H. M. Hake) London, 1908–25.

Bromley and Child, 1960 – J. Bromley and H. Child, *The Armorial Bearings of the Guilds of London*, London 1960.

CA. – W. H. Godfrey, A. R. Wagner, H. Stanford London, *The College of Arms* (16th Monograph of the London Survey Committee), London, 1963.

Christensen, 1940 – S. F. Christensen, *Kongedragterne fra 17. og 18. Aarhundrede*, Copenhagen, 1940.

Croft-Murray and Hulton, 1960 – E. Croft-Murray and P. Hulton, *Catalogue of British Drawings vol. 1: XVI and XVII Centuries*, London (British Museum), 1960.

Dalton, 1909 – O. M. Dalton, *Catalogue of the Ivory Carvings of the Christian Era*, London (British Museum), 1909.

Dalton, 1912 – O. M. Dalton, *Franks Bequest. Catalogue of the Finger Rings*, London (British Museum), 1912.

Denholm-Young, 1965 – N. Denholm-Young, *History and Heraldry 1254 to 1310*, Oxford, 1965.

Dennys, 1975 – R. Dennys, *The Heraldic Imagination*, London, 1975.

Druitt, 1906 – H. Druitt, *A Manual of Costume as Illustrated by Monumental Brasses*, London, 1906.

Dugdale, 1953 – F. Maddison, D. Styles and A. Wood, *Sir William Dugdale 1605–1686*, Warwick, 1953.

Eames, 1968 – E. Eames, *Medieval Tiles A Handbook*, London (British Museum), 1968.

Eden, 1934 – F. S. Eden, 'Heraldic Parliament Rolls', *The Connoisseur*, xciv (1934), pp. 363–66.

Ffoulkes, 1912 – C. Ffoulkes, 'Jousting Cheques of the Sixteenth Century', *Archaeologia*, lxiii (1912), pp. 31–50.

Fletcher, 1895 – W. Y. Fletcher, *English Bookbindings in the British Museum*, London, 1895.

Gauthier, 1972 – M-M. Gauthier, *Émaux du moyen âge occidental*, Fribourg, 1972.

G.E.C. – G. E. Cokayne, *The Complete Peerage*, 13 vols., new and rev. ed., London, 1910–40.

Griggs, 1887 – W. Griggs, *Illustrations of Armorial China*, London, 1887.

Guide, 1924 – British Museum, *A Guide to the Mediaeval Antiquities and Objects of Later Date*, London, 1924.

HCEC. – London, College of Arms, *Catalogue of the Heralds' Commemorative Exhibition 1484–1934*, London, 1936.

Hobson, 1903 – R. L. Hobson, *Catalogue of the Collection of English Pottery*, London (British Museum), 1903.

Hobson, 1905 – R. L. Hobson, *Catalogue of the Collection of English Porcelain*, London (British Museum), 1905.

Hobson, 1910 – R. L. Hobson, *Worcester Porcelain*, London, 1910.

Hobson, 1923 – R. L. Hobson, *Catalogue of the Frank Lloyd Collection of Worcester Porcelain*, London (British Museum), 1923.

Hodgkin, 1891 – J. C. Hodgkin, *Examples of Early English Pottery*, London, 1891.

Howard, 1974 – D. S. Howard, *Chinese Armorial Porcelain*, London, 1974.

Hunter Blair, 1943 – C. H. Hunter Blair, 'Armorials upon English Seals from the Twelfth to the Sixteenth Centuries', *Archaeologia*, lxxxix (1943), pp. 1–26.

Landon, 1935 – L. Landon, *The Itinerary of King Richard I*, Pipe Roll Soc., New Series, xiii (1935).

Linecar and Stone, 1968 – H. W. A. Linecar and A. G. Stone, *English Proof and Pattern Crown-sized Pieces 1658–1960*, London, 1968.

Macklin, 1913 – H. W. Macklin, *The Brasses of England*, 3rd ed., London, 1913.

Marshall, 1946 – H. R. Marshall, 'Armorial Worcester Porcelain of the Dr. Wall Period 1751–83', *Transactions of the English Ceramic Circle*, 2, pt. 9 (1946), pp. 188–218.

Medallic Ill. – E. Hawkins, A. W. Franks and H. A. Grueber, *Medallic Illustrations of the History of Great Britain and Ireland*, 2 vols., London (British Museum), 1885, reprinted 1969.

Montague Guest Cat. – *Catalogue of the Montague Guest Collection of Badges, Tokens and Passes*, London (British Museum), 1930.

NPG., 1973 – London, National Portrait Gallery exhibition catalogue, *Richard III*, London, 1973.

Nevinson, 1948 – J. L. Nevinson, 'The Earliest Dress and Insignia of the Knights of the Garter', *Apollo*, xlvii (1948), pp. 80–83.

Nichols, 1845 – J. G. Nichols, *Examples of Decorative Tiles*, London, 1845.

Nickson, 1970 – M. A. E. Nickson, *Early Autograph Albums in the British Museum*, London, 1970.

Oman, 1974 – C. Oman, *British Rings 800–1914*, London, 1974.

Ottawa, 1972 – Ottawa, National Gallery of Canada exhibition catalogue, *Art and the Courts*, 1972.

Pine, 1730 – J. Pine, *The Procession and Ceremonies Observed at the Time of the Installation of the Knights Companions of the Most Honourable Military Order of the Bath, . . .*, London, 1730.

Rackham, 1936 – B. Rackham, *A Guide to the Collections of Stained Glass*, London (Victoria and Albert Museum), 1936.

Reading, 1963 – Reading Museum and Art Gallery catalogue, *Exhibition of Heraldry*, 1963.

Rickert, 1965 – M. Rickert, *Painting in Britain the Middle Ages*, 2nd ed., Harmondsworth, 1965.

Round, 1894 – J. H. Round, 'The Introduction of Armorial Bearings into England', *The Archaeological Journal*, li (1894), pp. 43–48.

SAHE. Society of Antiquaries, *Illustrated Catalogue of the Heraldic Exhibition, 1894*, London, 1896.

Scott, 1976 – K. L. Scott, *The Caxton Master and his Patrons*, Cambridge Bibliographical Society Monograph no. 8, Cambridge, 1976.

Smith Ellis, 1869 – W. Smith Ellis, *The Antiquities of Heraldry*, London, 1869.

Stanford London, 1956 – H. Stanford London, *Royal Beasts*, The Heraldry Society, 1956.

Stanford London, 1970 – H. Stanford London, *The Life of William Bruges*, Harleian Society, cxi–cxii (1959–60), 1970.

Stephenson, 1903 – M. Stephenson, *A List of Palimpsest Brasses in Great Britain*, London, 1903.

Stephenson, 1926 – M. Stephenson, *A List of Monumental Brasses in the British Isles*, London, 1926.

Tilley, 1967 and 1968 – F. Tilley, 'London City Company Arms on English Delftware, Parts I–III', *The Antique Collector*, (1967), pp. 124–29, 265–71; (1968), pp. 125–30.

Tonnochy, 1952 – A. B. Tonnochy, *Catalogue of British Seal-dies in the British Museum*, London, 1952.

Tudor-Craig, 1925 – A. Tudor-Craig, *Armorial Porcelain of the Eighteenth Century*, London, 1925.

Wagner, 1939 – A. R. Wagner, *Historic Heraldry of Britain*, Oxford, 1939.

Wagner, 1946 – A. R. Wagner, *Heraldry in England*, London, 1946.

Wagner, 1956 – A. R. Wagner, *Heralds and Heraldry in the Middle Ages*, 2nd ed., Oxford, 1956.

Wagner, 1967 – A. R. Wagner, *Heralds of England*, London, 1967.

Wagner, 1972 – A. R. Wagner, *English Genealogy*, 2nd ed., Oxford, 1972.

Wagner and Sainty, 1967 – A. R. Wagner and J. C. Sainty, 'The Origin of the Introduction of Peers in the House of Lords', *Archaeologia*, ci (1967), pp. 119–50.

Waller, 1975 – J. G. and L. A. B. Waller, *Monumental Brasses* (reprinted with corrections and additions by J. A. Goodall), London, 1975.

Whitcomb, 1956 – N. Whitcomb, *Medieval Floor Tiles of Leicestershire*, Leicester, 1956.

Whitton, 1949–51 – C. A. Whitton, 'The Coinage of Henry VIII and Edward VI in Henry's Name', *British Numismatic Journal*, xxvi (1949–51), pp. 56–89, 171–212.

Windsor, 1975 – Windsor, St George's Chapel, *The Quincentenary Handbook*, 1975.

Wright, 1973 – C. E. Wright, *English Heraldic Manuscripts in the British Museum*, London, 1973.

Index of Names

(whose arms and badges occur in the Catalogue)